Making Schools Work

SUCESSFUL SCHOOLS
Guidebooks to Effective Educational Leadership
Fenwick W. English, Series Editor

1 MAPPING EDUCATIONAL SUCCESS
   Strategic Thinking and Planning for School Administrators
   Roger Kaufman

2 SHAPING SCHOOL POLICY
   Guide to Choices, Politics, and Community Relations
   Karen S. Gallagher

3 AVOIDING LEGAL HASSLES
   What School Administrators *Really* Need to Know
   William A. Streshly, Larry E. Frase

4 DECIDING WHAT TO TEACH AND TEST
   Developing, Aligning, and Auditing the Curriculum
   Fenwick W. English

5 MAXIMIZING PEOPLE POWER IN SCHOOLS
   Motivating and Managing Teachers and Staff
   Larry E. Frase

6 MEETING THE NEEDS OF SPECIAL STUDENTS
   Legal, Ethical, and Practical Ramifications
   Lawrence J. Johnson, Anne M. Bauer

7 MAKING SCHOOLS WORK
   Practical Management of Support Operations
   William K. Poston, Jr., M. Paula Stone, Connie Muther

8 POWER TO THE SCHOOLS
   School Leader's Guidebook to Restructuring
   William J. Bailey

9 LEADING INTO THE 21st CENTURY
   Fenwick W. English, Larry E. Frase, Joanne M. Arhar

MAKING SCHOOLS WORK

Practical Management of Support Operations

William K. Poston, Jr.
M. Paula Stone
Connie Muther

CORWIN PRESS, INC.
A Sage Publications Company
Newbury Park, California

Copyright © 1992 by Corwin Press, Inc.

All rights reserved. No part of this book may be reproduced or utilized in any form or by any means, electronic or mechanical, including photocopying, recording, or by any information storage and retrieval system, without permission in writing from the publisher.

The graphics and forms from Connie Muther in Chapter 4 appeared first in *Textbook Adoption*, copyright © 1983, 1992, by Connie Muther. Reprinted by permission of Textbook Adoption Advisory Services, Inc.

For information address:

Corwin Press, Inc.
A Sage Publications Company
2455 Teller Road
Newbury Park, California 91320

SAGE Publications Ltd.
6 Bonhill Street
London EC2A 4PU
United Kingdom

SAGE Publications India Pvt. Ltd.
M-32 Market
Greater Kailash I
New Delhi 110 048 India

Printed in the United States of America

Library of Congress Cataloging-in-Publication Data

Poston, William K., Jr.
  Making schools work: practical management of support operations / William K. Poston, Jr., M. Paula Stone, Connie Muther.
    p. cm.—(Successful schools; v. 7)
  Includes bibliographical references.
  ISBN 0-8039-6016-6 (pb)
  1. School management and organization—United States. I. Stone, M. Paula. II. Muther, Connie. III. Title. IV. Series.
LB2805.P734 1992   92-3073
                                                                                                   CIP

99 00 01 02 03 04 05 10 9 8 7 6 5 4 3 2

Corwin Press Production Editor: Tara S. Mead

Contents

Foreword		ix
Fenwick W. English		
Preface		xi
About the Authors		xvii
1.	Fostering School Quality With Community and Staff Involvement	1
	1.1 A Commonwealth of Investors in the School's Mission	2
	1.2 Foundations: Partnerships for External Funding for School Improvement	10
	1.3 Maximizing Student Achievement Through Volunteer Programs and Alternative Staffing	11
	1.4 Setting up a Volunteer Program to Enhance Student Learning	15
	1.5 Dissemination of Information to Gain Support for Schools	17
	1.6 Accountability in School-Community Relations	20
	1.7 Summary	21

2. Scheduling and Configuring Schools for Achievement — 22

    Chapter Organization — 23
    2.1 Scheduling Instructional Time to Extend Academic Learning — 24
    2.2 Designing Flexible Grouping Patterns of Staff and Students — 29
    2.3 Accessing Special Programs and Services for Widely Diverse Students — 35
    2.4 Evaluating Administrative Duties in Organizing Schools for Achievement — 40
    2.5 Summary — 40
    References — 42

3. Providing Sound Ancillary Services for Effective Schools — 43

    3.1 Ancillary Services Defined — 44
    3.2 Ancillary Services: Scope of Support and Assistance — 44
    3.3 Risk Management — 45
    3.4 Office Management — 47
    3.5 Transportation — 49
    3.6 Food Services — 53
    3.7 Enterprise Operations — 57
    3.8 Expansion of Support — 58
    3.9 Privatization — 59
    3.10 Summary — 62
    References — 63

4. Selecting Instructional Materials That Work and Avoid Censorship Challenges — 64

    4.1 Decisions to Make Before Beginning — 65
    4.2 Developing the Materials Selection Process Plan — 68
    4.3 Organizing Publisher Data to Get Down to the Best Three — 83
    4.4 Working With Publishers' Representatives and Handling Sample Materials — 85
    4.5 Conducting the In-Depth Evaluation — 87
    4.6 Selecting the Best Publisher — 89

4.7	Presenting the Recommendation to the School Board for Approval	89
4.8	Handling Challenges to Selected Materials	90
4.9	Implementing the Use of the New Materials	90
4.10	Assuring Selected Materials Will Work	91
4.11	Library Standards and Management	93
4.12	Summary	94
	References	95

5. Assuring a Safe and Orderly School Environment — 96

5.1	Issues in Creating Safe and Secure Schools	97
5.2	Overview: The Research and Rationale for Safe Schools	98
5.3	Summary	106
	References	109

6. Planning, Improving, and Maintaining School Facilities — 110

6.1	Facilities and Educational Quality	111
6.2	Facilities Management	111
6.3	Evaluating School Facilities	112
6.4	Facility Planning	114
6.5	Selecting an Architect	118
6.6	Stewardship and Care of Facilities and Resources	119
6.7	Energy Management	122
6.8	Summary	124
	References	124

7. Broadening Computer Technology Functions for Quality Schools — 125

7.1	Uses of Computer Technology in Schools	126
7.2	Major Application Program Options	127
7.3	Instructional Support and Assistance	130
7.4	Word Processing and Desktop Publishing	135
7.5	Spreadsheets and Accounting	136
7.6	Data Base Management	139
7.7	Graphics Presentation, Painting, and Drawing	141
7.8	Communications	143

	7.9 Programs and Application Development	144
	7.10 Selecting Computer Hardware	147
	7.11 Moving Schools Into the Technological Future	152
	7.12 Summary	153
	References	153
8.	School-Based Budgeting for Cost Efficiency and Educational Effectiveness	155
	8.1 Enhancing Productivity in Use of Resources	156
	8.2 School-Based Budgeting	158
	8.3 Budgeting Processes and Levels	162
	8.4 Implementing School-Based Performance Budgeting	165
	8.5 Moving Toward Performance Budgeting	169
	8.6 Organizational Benefits of Performance Budgeting	174
	8.7 Summary	175
	References	176
Troubleshooting Guide		177

Foreword

While education is relatively simple, schools are quite complex organizations. These two facts are often confusing to the public. How many administrators have been queried by naive community members with, "What do you do in the summer?" The assumption behind the question implies that, once teaching stops, what else is there?

This volume by Bill Poston, Paula Stone, and Connie Muther tackles some of the most important functions school administrators must perform wisely: interacting with the local community in building support for an individual school building (a critical ingredient in making site-based management really work); upgrading technology in schools; selecting the mainstay of all educational tools, the textbook; keeping schools safe and orderly places for children; operating a quality food service program; and applying and using sound budgeting techniques. In short, this book deals with the very practical management tools school leaders must master to practice the art of leadership. They are as essential to school administration as any basic skills would be to any person engaged in managing a complex and costly human institution providing a public service to a local population, with national implications. Experienced school administrators know that, unless a school is fiscally sound, the administrators won't last very long. They also come to recognize the unalterable importance of a strong textbook adoption process to provide the bedrock focus of their instructional program.

Yet, the newer technological revolution has left few places in society untouched with its pervasive influence. Children, with Nintendo experience, often have more dexterity and knowledge of technology than their teachers. The fear of computers still exists in many schools. For schools to remain educationally viable and provide linkages to a world in which students will live and compete, however, they must use technology much more soundly than they have in the past.

I'm confident the school practitioner will find this volume on the essential school support services to be of great assistance in being responsive to the consistent and yet changing conditions affecting schools today.

The authors are seasoned school practitioners with wide national experience in school affairs. The lead author, Bill Poston of Iowa State University, served as a superintendent of schools for 17 years and was the youngest elected president of Phi Delta Kappa, the educational fraternity, in its history. Coauthors Paula Stone and Connie Muther have also enjoyed national visibility: Stone in curriculum auditing, and Muther in performing staff development sessions for such organizations as the ASCD (Association of Supervision and Curriculum Development) in textbook selection and adoption. I am pleased their combined expertise could be combined into this very small, but immensely practical volume.

FENWICK W. ENGLISH
University of Kentucky

Preface

There is more to a quality school than meets the eye. Perhaps you've heard the old maxim: "All you need for a good school is a log with a dedicated teacher on one end and a diligent student on the other." Well, it isn't that simple. For instance, the log would have to be located and obtained for the teacher. It would have to meet certain specifications, such as being located under a cover of shade. Someone would have to clean off the bark and branches to make it comfortable, and someone would have to keep the area around the log clean for safety and protection from potential nuisances like poison ivy. Someone would have to transport the student from home to the log on time for school; someone else would have to be sure the student has a good lunch at midday; and someone else would have to keep track of the subjects covered and units accumulated. In addition, someone would have to select and gather learning materials, and so on and so forth.

You get the picture—there are many "behind-the-scenes" responsibilities that can make or break the chances for success of any school. School organizations need support people and services to be effective and to succeed in their basic mission of teaching and learning. A few examples can expand upon the point. Consider these situations:

- Your school needs to upgrade instruction and management operations with computers. What equipment and software should you buy?
- Teachers report the need for a new text in language arts. How do you find and choose the best option?
- Your school has just found that financial revenues are declining for next year. How can you protect educational priorities?
- Your community has approved the construction of an addition to your school. How do you make sure the new space will meet your educational needs?
- Your school's food service program is losing money and is taking funds away from instruction. What options are available to you?
- Parents and teachers are complaining about vandalism and violence at your school. How do you create and maintain a safe and orderly school environment?

If you are like most school administrators, your long suit is in the area of instruction. After all, your training probably prepared you first as a teacher. Now, instructional supervision is your prime responsibility, and producing teaching and learning is the main reason for your school's existence. Lack of appropriate support services and activities, however, can hamper the effective delivery of instruction. Without sound and beneficial support services, attainment of the school's primary mission may be jeopardized and the school may fail.

Defining Support Services

Support services take many forms in schools. Primarily, support services are the processes that help supply your school with the necessities and means needed to function and operate. The key terms here are *help, supply,* and *means.* A support service is an act or instance of *helping* your school to accomplish its mission. Schools, to exist and subsist, must be *supplied* with the *means* necessary for them to fulfill their societal charge and obligations. Means needed can be time, money or resources, relationships, people, materiel, or anything by which a wanted goal or end can be accomplished or achieved.

In selecting the specific support services to feature in this book, major consideration was given to those services and activities that are important in helping your school accomplish its mission. In addition, those areas of responsibility that are outside the mainstream of educational administrator preparation programs were most often given special attention.

The Need for This Book

The intent of this book is to be of practical help to busy school administrators. The organization of the book should give you, the practicing administrator, three things: knowledge you can use, insights and tools appropriate to your job, and time-saving ways and means to get and keep a quality school.

Many of us in school administration learned the complexities and considerations that constitute effective school management the hard way—on the job. Applications of research and experience from others should help us find shortcuts to effective school practice. Consequently, this book is designed and organized to help you learn what it takes to find and use the right ways and means to optimize support services for a successful school. The knowledge and information included were selected carefully to give you what you need and can use to do your job better.

This book is intended to reach several audiences: school principals, assistant principals, school superintendents, school business managers, school directors and executives, students of educational administration, and anyone interested in proficient school management. It is very difficult to run a school well, and the insights provided in this book can show you new and more powerful ways to make your difficult job easier.

The information in this book should save you time. In managing effective school districts, support services and activities often account for as much as half (or even more) of administrative time and management responsibilities. Sometimes, excessive time spent upon managing support services can conflict with instructional duties and obligations. Successful management demands efficiency in planning and organizing, and it also requires a broad and deep knowledge and an appreciation of many events, circumstances, and activities that affect performance. Yet, often, little is known about the diverse functions and tasks needed to run a school well and the way to get greater production within time constraints. In effect, this book aims at helping you fulfill the many support responsibilities in managing a school efficiently so you will be able to spend more of your valuable time and energy on the school's primary mission of instruction.

The Plan of This Book

The scope of the book is "lean and mean." It is not a huge tome with comprehensive detail; it is a carefully thought out, pithy, and succinct compilation of high-priority information in support services. This book is an effort to explain several key areas of support service and to show how to provide them efficiently and effectively in your school. There is much to learn, but what the book provides is significant. The approach is to introduce the demands in each area of service, to apply findings from research and experience practically, and to show useful ways to meet the obligations of school management with a minimum of headaches.

Chapter 1 deals with maximizing the involvement of people in accomplishing the work of the school. No school ever has enough help, or people, to do all of the things it needs to do perfectly. Clever administrators, however, have learned many ways to extend the programs and services of their school with community involvement and school-community partnerships. This chapter shows you how to create and implement effective programs for extending instruction and pupil achievement through the use of volunteers, alternate staffing, unique community support, and effective relationships.

Preface

Chapter 2 addresses how to configure your school for achievement. Arranging people, time, and facilities often can be a nuisance to school administrators, and this chapter helps you meet the challenge and organize resources for productive and constructive use. This chapter shows you how to meet the diverse needs of diverse students, how to manage school factors to expand learning opportunities, and how to help obtain comprehensive and accessible services for productive schooling.

Chapter 3 applies itself to operating successful ancillary services, including food service, transportation, risk management, office administration, and enterprise operations. It describes how to administer responsibilities in developing and delivering ancillary programs and activities. This chapter helps to reduce burdensome work, boost school capabilities, and resolve problems and issues. A highlight of this chapter is the helpful section on enterprise operations, an often neglected but important aspect of school management.

Chapter 4 provides powerful processes and procedures to help find, evaluate, and select textbooks and instructional materials. It suggests planning cycles, outlines review and selection criteria, defines task responsibilities, and describes powerful evaluation techniques for use with instructional materials. With this valuable information, you will be more able to make, support, evaluate, and defend selections of instructional texts, supplementary matter, and other teaching and learning materials.

Chapter 5 outlines how to configure and obtain productive pupil behavior, safe school environments, positive school climate, and instructional integrity in schools. The chapter provides you with a focus on administrative actions that produce not only a safe and orderly school but a school that produces effective achievement. Policies, procedures, checklists, and indicators are described for convenience and in appropriate detail.

Chapter 6 deals with planning, organizing, constructing, and managing school facilities. The emphasis is on improving facility plans, resources, and requirements for quality instruction. In addition, helpful direction is given on how to exercise good stewardship of school facilities, resources, and environments as well as on how to match facilities with educational needs.

Chapter 7 provides and expands understanding of ways to use technology for effective schools. Administrators need to know what computers and other forms of technology are and what they mean for education from the perspective of instruction and management. Administrators will find this chapter very helpful in evaluating the level of effectiveness in their own school's use of technology and also should find many suggestions on how to augment school programs and services with technology.

Chapter 8 addresses school-based budgeting and how to manage resources for productivity. Every administrator faces the challenge of conserving resources while meeting higher expectations. You'll find several sound strategies for meeting new program needs with existing or declining financial support. The curriculum-driven budget is explained, including ways to use performance results in budget decision making.

What This Book Offers

Throughout the book, important research and thought in school management is referenced. While much of this material is ignored in major educational journals, it has much to offer to the school practitioner who seeks quality in all aspects of his or her school. The establishment of quality is not so much a destination as it is a journey. The search for quality and excellence across the broad spectrum of administrative responsibilities in schools never ends. This book works to bring administrative practitioners a few steps closer to the end of their quest for quality and productivity. If it succeeds in part, our work was well worth the effort.

WILLIAM K. POSTON, JR.
Iowa State University
M. PAULA STONE
Mankato State University
CONNIE MUTHER
Textbook Adoption Advisory Services

About the Authors

William K. Poston, Jr., senior author, is Associate Professor and Section Leader of Educational Administration in the College of Education at Iowa State University of Science and Technology. He is a graduate of the University of Northern Iowa, and his graduate degrees are from Arizona State University. His professional background includes extensive teaching, research, and public school administration, and his background is uniquely rich with international travel and professional organization participation. He was the youngest elected international president to serve Phi Delta Kappa, the honor fraternity in education, and he was selected as one of 75 Outstanding Young Educators in America in 1981. He has served as an educational researcher, school principal, and assistant superintendent. He also served for 15 years in the superintendency of school districts in Tucson, Arizona; Billings, Montana; and Phoenix-Tempe, Arizona. After 25 years in public school administration, he joined Drake University as Associate Professor and Department Chair in Educational Administration, prior to joining the faculty at Iowa State University in fall 1990. He is an active lecturer and educational consultant across the country, and he conducts seminars and training in curriculum auditing and performance-based budgeting for the American Association of School Administrators. Author of many professional journal articles and other publications, he is currently writing another book, *Curriculum-Driven Budgeting.*

M. Paula Stone is Associate Professor of Educational Administration at Mankato State University in Minnesota. She is a graduate of the University of San Francisco, and her graduate degrees are from the University of Washington and Seattle University. Her professional background includes teaching and school administration, and she has been a school principal, director of curriculum and staff development, and assistant superintendent. After serving more than 25 years in teaching and administration in schools in California, Saskatchewan, Washington, Massachusetts, and Arizona, she joined the faculty at Mankato State University in 1990. She is an active educational researcher and was awarded a special faculty research grant her first year in the professorship to study the effects of educational administrator competency. She is active in professional organizations and conducts seminars and in-service training for school administrators on topics dealing with school reform and transformational leadership. She is an active writer and counts many articles and other professional writings among her publications.

Connie Muther is Director of Textbook Adoption Advisory Services, a professional service consulting firm, located in Manchester, Connecticut. The firm is considered unrivaled in providing training and materials for school practitioners in textbook and instructional material selection and evaluation. A nationally known consultant, author, and speaker, she is active in curriculum development and the creation of effective and valid instructional materials. Hundreds of school districts employ her materials and processes for the improvement of instruction. She has extensive experience with all major aspects of publishing and education and has been a classroom teacher and a coordinator of curriculum and instruction. She is the creator of the video production, *The Pitfalls of Textbook Adoption,* produced by the Association for Supervision and Curriculum Development (ASCD). Her articles appear regularly in *Educational Leadership* and other professional journals. She recently was sponsored by Phi Delta Kappa International to conduct a national series on ways to improve instruction and learning. Her views have been featured by the media, including *U.S. News and World Report, The Christian Science Monitor,* and *Education Week.*

1

Fostering School Quality With Community and Staff Involvement

A school is a reflection of the community it serves. At the same time, a community is a reflection of its schools. The quality of any community is inextricably interwoven with the quality of its schools, and vice versa. The community is a powerhouse of support and human resources for the schools, and it is also the largest stakeholder in the schools. It provides the clients, pays the salaries, and funds operations. It votes in and out board members and writes letters to the newspaper editor. The community is both critic of and provider for its schools. It gives generously in times of plenty but holds the line in lean times.

Nothing is closer to the heart of the community than its schools, and nothing is more powerful than the community for creating a dynamic school system. Schools need their community to be all that they can be. A community's goodwill and favor alone are powerful enough to move a "fair" school to be a "good" one and a "good" school to be a "great" one. Many administrators have discovered the formula: Connect with the community. Build two-way channels of communication. Bring in the community and move the school out among the community. Integrate, collaborate, and communicate!

This chapter focuses on five areas for today's administrators who want to create quality schools through productive relationships with the community. It describes administrative actions for enhanced school-community relations and outlines how to create school-business partnerships to improve schools. Student achievement improvement is shown with volunteer programs, and getting your school's message out is encouraged to gain public support for your school. In addition, you will learn how to gain accountability in school-community relations programs.

1.1 A Commonwealth of Investors in the School's Mission

Participants in the educational mission nowadays encompass far more than district-hired professional and classified staff. Today, administrators can view the educational enterprise as a commonwealth of shareholders, as illustrated in Figure 1.1. In addition to professional staff and parents, several segments of the community have interest in the effectiveness of the school in educating youth.

The many shareholders in the mission of the school have expanded from a few (parents and teachers) to a larger number of interested parties. Furthermore, interested parties may play several roles, that is, parent, volunteer, taxpayer, and so on. Participative community life today emphasizes inter- and intra-relationships among various roles in the community. By keeping in mind the collaborative nature of contemporary community life, administrators can work successfully with the community in educating youth.

Community and Staff Involvement

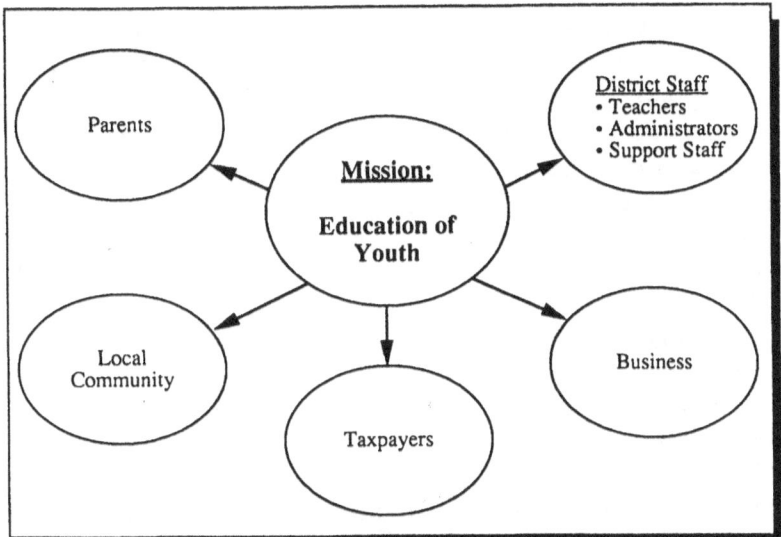

Figure 1.1. Shareholders in the School's Mission

A. *Administrative Actions for Enhancing School-Community Relationships*

Although you can't possibly please everyone in your community, as an administrator you must keep a high average. Administrators who don't will leave—one way or another. While independence and being "your own man or woman" were characteristics of self-reliant pioneers and rangers on the open plains, life nowadays requires an interdependent mind-set. The community sees its school as an extension of itself and wants to have a "professional family" relationship with it. The community wants the school to stand for something, and it also wants to be part of what it stands for, not an outsider to it.

Administrative functions in fostering school-community relations are both expressive and reflective. For example, before you can "stand and deliver" excellent public relations programs, you must "sit and design" their objectives, time lines, resource allocations, and evaluation techniques. "Shooting from the hip" used to be acceptable standard operating procedure in past times and places (including in school administration), but if that approach is used nowadays for school-community relations, the administrator may find an unsympathetic community and school board. Underplanning for public relations and overestimating the tolerance of the community for such may leave the unwary administrator without credibility and without a powerful ally in the school-community partnership.

Administering programs that enhance school-community relationships requires four basic managerial actions:

Data gathering
Planning
Communicating
Evaluating

These four actions can apply to any goals or programs the administrator has for implementation. But, although they appear to be commonplace, they are not always common administrative practice—except in the cases of successful school administrators!

B. *Building School-Business Partnerships to Improve Schools*

Your schools can benefit from school-business partnerships in a variety of ways. Although funding and material capital are surely part of them, more compelling is the moral support that business partnerships can provide. When business is a part of the school's mission, students will have advocates. Business can and wants to be a participant in the educational mission and enterprise. The moral support of the business community is an invaluable resource for schools because the bonds that connect the schools with such a group increase the school's strength of purpose. Administrators can view business as key shareholders in the school. Business views its relationship with schools as a means of accomplishing public service and improving the future work force. By joining forces in an alliance, both school and business can magnify their unique contributions to the school's mission.

c. Administrative Readiness and Data Gathering

To begin a school-business partnership, the first step is to identify your intended outcomes. Be crystal clear about your purposes for forming a partnership. Clarity of intent will keep you on track as you plan, implement, and evaluate your efforts. So, the question is this: "Why do you want to form a school-business partnership?" Your answer may include one or more of the following purposes:

- To broaden goodwill and support for the school
- To tap funding and/or material resources for the school
- To correct perceived misunderstandings about the school
- To exchange resources between school and business
- To obtain outside talent and expertise
- To publicize the school's accomplishments
- To solicit political support for controversial programs
- To broaden staff's view about important school goals
- To increase student motivation for curricular subjects
- To extend student opportunities for application of skills
- To raise student aspirations for career goals and opportunities
- To improve the school's image in the eyes of community leaders
- To give business a resource
- To enrich the school's curriculum
- To reinforce classroom instruction

Once your outcomes have been clearly identified, you are ready to select the form of partnership that suits your needs and purposes. Business partnerships with the schools take many forms and some of the most typical are listed below:

- Adopt-a-School programs
- Internships
- Apprenticeships
- Career awareness programs
- Staff development programs
- Long-range planning consultancies

- Trustee or board membership
- Task force membership
- Advisory or consultant services
- Classroom speakers
- Field trip resources

These types of relationships with the business community exist currently in many districts across the country. Rather than having to "reinvent the wheel," an administrator can select any of the above forms and initiate action to realize a productive partnership. Some of them are more common at the secondary level, such as internships and apprenticeships, while field trip resources, classroom speakers, and Adopt-a-School programs are found at both elementary and secondary levels. Some of them also address the inclusion of the community in decision-making or planning efforts, such as advisory and task force membership.

The form of business partnership you want to have for your school also depends on what resources you have in your community. Collect specific data that will answer the following questions:

1. Which businesses in the community have supported schools in the past?
2. Which businesses have services you already know could be used by the school?
3. Have teachers ever indicated special interest in particular business agencies?
4. Have parents indicated specific business connections with the school?
5. What response did you get by speaking with key business personnel?
6. How do teachers and support staff feel about managing a partnership?

Other techniques you can use to find out what potential business resources are include the following:

- At the next faculty meeting, ask staff to brainstorm businesses that they think may be interested in partnerships.

- Ask influential parents if they know any business people in the community who may be interested.
- Review past issues of the local newspaper to identify possible businesses.
- Place an "ad" in your newsletter (or the local newspaper) indicating interest in establishing a school-business partnership.
- Use the yellow pages of the telephone book and check off potential partners.

Typical partnerships across the country are from the local private sector and include banks, service clubs, sports teams, restaurants, book publishing companies, bookstores, industrial companies, law firms, individual volunteers, and hospitals. Your inquiry and data gathering will identify the resources your community offers.

D. Administrative Planning: The Blueprint for Results

Now that your purposes, types of partnerships, and resources have been identified, you are ready to apply the action that will be the blueprint for realizing results. Here's the point of difference between those who merely "talk" about an alliance with business and those who actually "walk the talk": a written planning document specifying the objective, key events, time lines, persons responsible, resources allocated, and evaluation. Although the possession of such a plan does not guarantee results, it is a powerful means for increasing the likelihood of positive results. Table 1.1 displays a typical planning form to reach the desired goal. This action plan is an example of how to specify the goal, key events, time line, persons responsible, resources needed, and evidence for evaluation in forming a partnership with business. Note that a *written* document, with clearly designated persons responsible and time lines established, is the key. Resources must be accurately specified, and evaluation techniques must consist of documented evidence on how each key event will be accomplished. Without built-in accountability, your most ambitious efforts can lose credibility. Table 1.1 spells out an example of administrative goal setting and action planning

TABLE 1.1 Sample Action Plan for Volunteer Speaker Program

Key Events	Time Line	Responsibility	Resources Needed	Evaluation
1. Meet with staff to identify needs and interest areas.	May 15	Principal and Department Chairs	Meeting time	Log of meeting indicating time, date, and summary (to be attached)
2. Contact potential business partners through letters, phone, visits.	August 15	Principal, Secretary, Department Chairs	Mailing materials	Written list of contacts and their responses (to be attached)
3. Meeting with potential business partners to clarify and exchange views.	August 29	Principal and Department Chairs	Meeting time and supplies	Documented meeting log—date, time, participants' names, summary (to be attached)
4. Final list of resource speakers compiled by name and topic.	September 8	Principal and Secretary	—	List of speakers document (to be attached)
5. Meeting with teachers to develop logistics of scheduling speakers.	September 10	Principal and Department Chairs	Meeting time	Log documenting meeting date, time, summary (to be attached)
6. Schedule sent to speakers.	September 12	Principal and Secretary	Mailing materials	Schedule form (to be attached)
7. Evaluation of speakers form developed.	September 30	Principal and Teachers	Meeting time	Forms and summary of results (to be attached)
8. First quarter evaluation of program.	November 10	Principal and Teachers	Evaluation forms and time	Forms and summary of results (to be attached)
9. Spring evaluation of program.	March 15	Principal and Teachers	Evaluation forms and time	Forms and summary of results (to be attached)
10. Final evaluation of speakers program.	May 15	Principal, Teachers, and Business Partners	Evaluation forms, mailing materials	Final overall summary (to be attached)

to carry out the community relations project. The action-plan project illustrated involves resource speakers for enhancing classroom instruction.

E. Administrative Communication and Implementation

Your action plan is now your map and blueprint for carrying through your partnership endeavor. It's usually a good idea to delegate to a staff member the task of keeping track of the plan's accomplishment all along the way. This gives you support as well as invested commitment from the staff. At this point, your efforts will be focused on building trust, clearly communicating your plan, and following through on each key event. The following tips on developing school-community partnerships should be reflected in your action document:

- *Target*: identifying key opinion leaders
- *Contact*: making contacts with prospective partners
- *Time*: forming a partnership requires time to build trust
- *Anticipation*: readying staff and community for support
- *Continuity*: monitoring the project for momentum
- *Delegation*: involving staff in the enterprise for commitment
- *Style*: communicating clearly in appealing ways to capture attention

F. Evaluation: Evidence of Accomplishment

Documentation of the accomplishment of each key event gives you and others tangible proof that your plan is on schedule. Generally speaking, you want more than merely a checkoff indicator that is supposed to mean "event accomplished." In the eyes of others, your administrative competence is demonstrated in visible results and outcomes. Written documentation of each key event, such as an agenda indicating the date and time of a meeting with a list of members present and a summary of the meeting, is an excellent example of tangible evidence of accomplishment. Documentation should be attached to your plan as events occur.

1.2 Foundations: Partnerships for External Funding for School Improvement

Finding sources outside the district, state, local, and categorical treasuries can be a hit-and-miss affair. Some schools do receive outside financial assistance in innovative ways, however. During the past 10 years, foundations have increasingly emerged as a way to financially support public schools. They do not supplant state funding, but they do contribute financially in a variety of ways. Because of the legal restrictions on public schools in raising funds for profit and the limited allowance for carryover of funds from one year to the next, public schools have found that foundations are one means for the community to contribute to local school improvement. Foundations are officially not a part of the district but, through collaboration and joint purposes, can be an independent "partner." Similar to organizations like the PTA, their efforts and contributions are "private, nonpublic." They write bylaws, elect officers, establish accounting procedures in alignment with state and local requirements, apply for tax-exempt status, establish policies, and make decisions on how to raise money for schools. The forms foundations take include

- corporations that "adopt" a school;
- groups of business members, parents, and interested citizens who form their own private foundation; and
- alumni groups that organize themselves into a nonprofit foundation.

Typically, the principal or other designated official district staff members are advisory members on the foundation board, not voting members. The contributions that foundations provide can include scholarships, auction proceeds, ticket raffles, direct donations, and numerous other forms selected by the foundation. The range of their contributions has been documented from a few thousand dollars to well over $100,000.

1.3 Maximizing Student Achievement Through Volunteer Programs and Alternative Staffing

Volunteers are members of the community who have a vested interest in quality schools and put their time as well as their tax dollars into their investment. Volunteer programs are not new, as all administrators know. But, like many components of daily school life, volunteer programs may be taken for granted, underused, and underestimated. On the other hand, many administrators have capitalized on their good fortune in being able to develop excellent volunteer programs. The benefits of having a solid, comprehensive program include increased student achievement, more focused instructional time for teachers, growth in self-esteem of volunteers, and decrease in student behavior problems. And never forget another potent benefit of a good volunteer program: increased understanding and support for the school's mission and activities. Although volunteers can participate in most areas of school life (see Figure 1.2), this section will elaborate on their value in helping teachers to maximize academic learning time for students in three ways:

1. tutoring students (under the supervision of a teacher);
2. handling custodial and clerical activities, thus freeing teachers to increase their time for teaching, prescription, and evaluation; and
3. enriching and extending classroom instruction through expert speakers on a focused topic.

You can organize a volunteer program both on a schoolwide level and/or on a classroom level. You may want to try out this approach with one or two teachers before introducing it as a schoolwide program. Figure 1.2 is a sample form to use for recruiting volunteers. It should be designed to fit the exact type of program your school is developing.

Name _____

Address _____

Home Phone _____

Work Phone _____

Areas for Volunteering

(Check [√] the items that apply.)

1. ☐ math tutor

2. ☐ reading tutor

3. ☐ writing and spelling tutor

4. ☐ general subjects tutor

5. ☐ playground

6. ☐ assistant supervisor

7. ☐ instructional team assistant

8. ☐ office clerical assistant

9. ☐ nurse assistant

10. ☐ computer tutor

11. ☐ other (specify: _____)

Identify your first, second, and third choices for days and times you can volunteer:

Monday ____ Tuesday ____ Wed. _____ Thurs. ____ Friday ____

Time _____ Time _____ Time _____ Time _____ Time _____

Comments:

Figure 1.2. Sample Volunteer Application Form

A. Volunteer Tutors for Maximizing Student Learning

Volunteers who have been appropriately trained in tutoring are an inestimable resource. They provide students with extended practice, corrective responses, and on-the-spot encouragement.

Whether in the classroom with the teacher or in another instructional setting, tutors can be an extension of the teacher's drill and practice routine. In addition, the tutor gives individualized encouragement and support to the student. While the tutor is working one-on-one or one-on-more, the teacher is freed to extend instruction to more students and to deliver higher-order instructional objectives. Caution: If students are to benefit fully, volunteers must receive training in *"how* to tutor *these* students in *these* subjects."* When such training is designed and delivered, student achievement and higher-order teaching increase. Classroom teachers also should be highly involved in this training of volunteers, in either a lead role or a participant role. Their acceptance of volunteers is absolutely critical to success.

B. Volunteer Custodial and Clerical Assistance

When volunteers assist in noninstructional tasks such as supervision of students and handling papers, teachers are freed to extend and heighten their professional instructional role. This usually translates to directing instruction to more students, additional time to teach, and additional time to design and evaluate programs. Caution: If students are going to benefit from the teacher having more time to do higher-order teaching and evaluating because the volunteers are taking care of clerical and supervisory duties, then the teaching and evaluating should really happen. You may have to be very explicit to staff about the purpose of volunteers in these roles and then monitor whether the extra time is really benefiting students directly.

C. Volunteers as Classroom Resource Speakers

Matching volunteer resource speakers to specific curriculum topics can be a dynamic and motivating way to enhance student learning. An alignment of the speaker's topic with the learning objective intended by the teacher must be designed in advance so that the occasion is not just another "time-filler" activity. Administrators are instrumental in setting up a vital, stimulating pool of resource speakers who can enhance student learning. The following steps should help in setting up a volunteer resource speaker program:

1. Request teachers to submit a list of topics for which they want resource speakers.
2. Compile your list of teacher requests by topics and by grade.
3. Brainstorm with the staff to find already known resources as well as potential speakers.
4. Write a letter to each of the persons or businesses on the "brainstormed" list requesting their expertise. Follow up with a phone call.
5. After you have received answers from your prospective speakers, compile your list by topic.
6. Distribute the list to the staff and ask for them to give you specific dates and times for having their speakers. Also request that they give you one to three learning objectives so that the speaker is aware of teachers' expectations for students.
7. Make arrangements far enough in advance for the speakers by scheduling them and requesting that they call the specific teacher for more information about the desired topic and objectives.
8. Give a certificate of appreciation to the speaker on the day of the scheduled appointment.
9. Have the teacher inconspicuously assess the quality of the speaker for future consideration.

D. *Volunteers and Alternative Staffing to Maximize Achievement*

Volunteers can also assist in allowing alternative staffing patterns that increase the intensity of basic skills instruction. The example that follows is one that some administrators in the country have tried successfully. By rearranging the sizes of various student groups taught throughout the day, you can give more intense instruction in basic skills areas to smaller groups. Basic skills classes—reading, math, language arts—can be reduced (e.g., to 15 students) if more teachers—regular and specialists—teach basics during a portion of the day. During the rest of the day, other classes, such as PE and music, would be larger (e.g., 35-40). In these larger classes, volunteers would act as tutors, supervisors, and monitors under the tutelage of the teacher. This plan (and variants of it) really does work, but it requires the commitment and flexibility of staff to "think outside the lines" of the traditional way to group students for instruction. Not all classes have to be 25-30 students every minute of the day, but staff must acknowledge this and be committed to trying alternative patterns of staffing. With support, their creativity will flourish and they may suggest a variety of staffing models. If only a few staff members are interested in this project, then you can capitalize on their risk taking and openness. They deserve your wholehearted support!

1.4 Setting up a Volunteer Program to Enhance Student Learning

Background administrative preparation for setting up a volunteer program includes the four processes of data gathering, planning, communication and implementation, and evaluation. The following steps should be helpful in establishing your volunteer program.

Data Gathering

1. Compute the number of volunteers you already have.
2. Solicit teacher attitudes and suggestions for the proposed volunteer program.
3. Review the budget for adequate funding and in-service resources for the program.

Planning

4. Define specific responsibilities for each of the volunteer roles, such as "student tutor," "custodial supervisor," or "classroom instructional clerk." By defining precisely the volunteer "student tutor's" responsibilities, you will avoid legal and educational problems that could arise involving student safety and professional job descriptions.
5. Plan training that closely matches the specific roles defined earlier. Anyone who is competent in designing training programs should be enlisted as soon as possible, because the training curriculum usually depends upon collaboration with teachers about their expectations and desires. This takes some time. The training should consist of the essential elements necessary for transfer, such as practice with coaching and feedback before actual performance in a classroom.
6. Design an appealing, persuasive volunteer recruitment program that specifies the areas needing assistance. Also emphasize that an "easy-to-learn" orientation program will be provided to volunteers on an ongoing basis. Plan a variety of recruitment techniques: speeches for senior citizens, spots on the local TV station, and so on.
7. Establish key event time lines, persons responsible, resources allocated, and evaluation techniques in a written format, as described earlier in this chapter.

Communication and Implementation

8. Now, launch your planned program according to the schedule you have established. Keep the momentum brisk and stimulating; follow up on "loose" threads.
9. Have a legal, inoffensive screening process for selecting volunteers. Not all volunteers may be sane, safe, moral, and competent enough to work with and near children.

Evaluation and Recognition

10. Provide a first-class recognition program for volunteers. The program should include written, oral, celebratory,

formal, and informal means of communication appreciation as well as sincere recognition of the volunteers' contributions.
11. Maintain ongoing assessment information about the program, such as numbers of volunteers, quality of volunteers, hours donated, types of services, time dedicated to training, and teachers' and students' attitudes about the program.
12. Revise the program as needed. Don't let current practice become the status quo. If something doesn't work, drop it and find a better way. Your persistence, enthusiasm, and organization are key to the success of your volunteer program enterprise!

1.5 Dissemination of Information to Gain Support for Schools

In the 1990s, administrators are expected to "have a vision" for their schools. In addition, the vision's ingredients are to be forms of "restructuring," "transformation," "excellence," "effectiveness," and other superlative notions. Writers also quickly added that, with the vision, there must be articulation skills, that is, "communication." A vision dies when it cannot be seen, heard, and relished.

A. Shared Vision and Communication

School-community relations are the administrator's vehicle for moving the school's vision out to the staff and community. Whether that vehicle is a Cadillac or a Chevy depends on the value administrators place on gaining support for their product. The vision itself may be strong and exemplary but, if the approach in communicating the vision is anemic, then all is in vain. A high-powered communication program tells the school's story and kindles the public's enthusiasm. The use of technology speeds up communication, connects the schools with a wider audience, and keeps track of audiences far more efficiently than traditional methods. Microcomputers, word processors, and cable television are revolutionary and immediately accessible. The key to good public relations is to tell the truth and tell it well! Use the checklist in the following section to do a quick scan of effective means of communication for telling your school's story and articulating your vision to the community.

B. School-Community Communications

To test your school-community communications quality, ask yourself the following question: "How frequently do I use the following techniques below in my school communications?"

Technique Used:	*For What?*
Graphic Designs	_____
Typesetting	_____
Desktop publishing	_____
Mailings	_____
Surveys	_____
Articles in newspapers	_____
Video productions	_____
Radio/TV spots	_____
Town meetings	_____
Telephone messages	_____
Special forums	_____
Commercial displays	_____
Community speeches	_____
Bumper stickers, buttons, T-shirts	_____
Billboards	_____
Closed circuit TV programs	_____
Brochures and newsletters	_____

Inclusion of the above communication techniques showcases your vision to a larger group of people. It can also keep staff focused on the mission and primary purpose of the school. The public is especially interested in your school's outcomes and the results of your educational endeavors. Keeping before the public the teaching-learning process gives a clear and salient message: "We are about the business of teaching and learning, and here's the evidence."

Suggestion. Design a highly concentrated series of media events that give the community an inside peek into the inner sanctum of the closed classroom. Let the public see, through a variety of media, the daily life of the classroom. This is a powerful perception-shaping technique that is a truthful picture of what school is all about. Let the public see teachers in the act of teaching and students responding and working together in learning activities. Let the public see students engaged in learning basic skills, creating artistic productions, solving scientific problems, and improving their citizenship behavior. These daily school activities may seem mundane to staff and students, but to the community, they give a message of confidence in the schools. The public expects both traditional and progressive approaches to instruction and, when they can see these occurring, they will believe in their schools. "Seeing is believing" is one of those "absolute truths" in the field of communications. The power of one documentary, for example, does more to shape public perception than a thousand speeches. Accessible high-tech equipment and techniques are invaluable gifts of the 1990s to administrators. One example is video production.

C. Video Productions of Teaching and Learning

Ask talented staff or outside volunteers to make a 10-minute video showcasing teaching and learning in the basic skills. Show your video to senior citizens and service clubs and broadcast it on the local TV station. Ask for public response to your video. You will get it! The response you receive is an indicator of public interest and support. Both critics and supporters will present their opinions, and those opinions will give you valuable information for future school-community relations planning. Using video production will yield long-range results that will dramatically affect the public's picture of your schools.

D. Public Speaking

Your professional image and skills in public speaking make a strong impression, for good or otherwise. Take the time to polish up—or overhaul—your speech-making skills. Join Toastmasters or some similar group that gives you personalized feedback. Your credibility and the school's are on the line every time you step up to the podium in formal and informal ways. Communication is the key instrument of your work, and your strength in that arena will make you a victor for community support.

1.6 Accountability in School-Community Relations

It is an axiom in administrative life that: "What gets measured gets done." By establishing an evaluation piece from the onset for any aspect of your community relations program, you are more likely to maintain focus and efficiently reach your objective. The four-step model described throughout this chapter—data gathering, planning, communication, and evaluation—demonstrates a way to materialize the "what gets measured gets done" axiom. The following list is practical and useful for administrators in keeping tabs on community relations' endeavors:

Surveys:	mailings
	telephone
	at on-site events
	in the newspaper
Statistics:	number of objectives accomplished
	number of volunteers
	number of complaints
	increase or decrease in scores, number of participants, and so on
Interviews:	formal
	informal
	staff
	targeted groups in community
	in person
	telephone
	video delivered on local TV station
Follow-ups:	internal debriefing after an event
	external opinions after an event
Communication audits:	comparison of internal and external perceptions on a variety of issues

The key for effective measurement of your community relations programs is to collect ongoing formal and informal information on a *regular* basis. In addition to building evaluation into your action plans, capitalize on regular school events to collect data, use the mail and high-tech services, and get in the habit of randomly scanning all segments of your community for their opinions.

1.7 Summary

Successful administrators capitalize on the community as a resource for support and assistance in carrying out the school's educational mission. Through proficient managerial planning and follow-through, you can advance the fostering of quality schools with the community. Four specific administrative actions you can use include data gathering, written action planning, communication and implementation of the plan, and evaluation. These actions can result in the acquisition of powerful allies in the community. Through school-business partnerships, the school gains human, material, and funding capital.

Volunteers can extend time-on-task by tutoring, relieving teachers of clerical tasks, and providing topical content to classroom instruction. Volunteers also fit into the design of alternative patterns of staffing by "teaming" with professional staff to assist in supervisory and noninstructional tasks. When you use high-tech forms of communication, you can target your messages both to specific and to widespread audiences. Keeping a pulse on how well the school is doing and how the community perceives the school requires you to have a variety of formal and informal means to evaluate program and public perception. You cannot build a great school alone—the school needs the community and the community needs the school!

2

Scheduling and Configuring Schools for Achievement

Experienced administrators have learned that, while there are numerous planks in the educational platform competing for attention, two in particular emerge as highly visible in building a solid foundation favoring academic achievement: time and personnel. As an administrator committed to the best outcomes for students, your efforts on their behalf entail keeping managerial focus on the arrangement of time and personnel. As is true for many aspects of school life, however, knowing what counts and implementing what counts may be very different enterprises. The truth is that we already have all the information we need to transform schools into communities of learners rather than sorting factories. The classroom research on effective teaching practices and models, the research on the negative effects of tracking, and the research on how teachers change all have been monumental contributions to our knowledge base for restructuring schools. Another fact, however, is that very few school districts and schools, for a variety of reasons, have been able to put this research into practice by changing structures, the way curriculum is delivered, and teacher in-service. This chapter will capitalize on the research that addresses the organization of time and staff and student groupings, with practical suggestions for implementation.

While effectively and creatively organizing time and personnel are critical conditions necessary for realizing our hopes and dreams for students, they also can be impediments to the same when organizational structures are weak or disunited. The challenge for administrators, therefore, is to summon the managerial creativity and organizational patterns that will result in the best use of the resources of time and personnel.

By dealing with the here-and-now realities of scheduling staff and time, administrators can truly be the difference between fulfilled or failed dreams of success for all students. Four key areas for maximizing time and personnel that dramatically affect pupil outcomes include (a) time, (b) student grouping, (c) special programs' accessibility, and (d) administrative duties affecting student achievement.

Chapter Organization

This chapter highlights four key areas in managing time and personnel to effect student achievement. The first is how to schedule instructional time to extend academic learning, followed by how to design flexible grouping patterns of staff and students to expand opportunities for pupils. Next, procedures for accessing special programs and services for widely diverse students are presented, and the chapter concludes with how you can evaluate your administrative duties to organize your school for achievement.

2.1 Scheduling Instructional Time to Extend Academic Learning

Of all the findings from educational research on how to increase pupil achievement, the most powerful finding to emerge concerns time. Time is the all-purpose element that embraces every aspect of school life. It is forever present but, once past, also forever gone. Because it is irretrievable, it is not surprising that the best teachers are those who get the most out of the time they have. "With-it" administrators also schedule and protect the largest possible amount of time dedicated to student academic learning. You may think that being so concerned with how time is used could destroy the climate of care and joy so necessary for nurturing students. On the contrary, schools that do master their time also jam-pack the time with quality experiences in which students both learn and enjoy. Because routine administrative responsibility includes bringing students, staff, and program together within a scheduled allotment of time, why not plan shrewdly so that those experiences can be savored longer within a longer academic time frame?

While excellent administrators are ever conscious and ever protective of time, this is not an easy task. As experienced administrators know, you are beset from all directions to compromise time. "All directions" refers to the staff, the students, the district office, the public, and even yourself. Because time is at the mercy of its users, a strong, unifying force is necessary to initiate and maintain maximum quantity and quality of time. Administrators are in the position to be that unifying force. Teachers, too, are at the mercy of numerous classroom interruptions that rob students of quality time. The more that time is scheduled for relevant learning, the more likely that learning will occur. The fewer the interruptions in academic learning time, the more that learning may occur. Many researchers have observed that only about 60% of a school day is actually available for instruction!

The list below identifies practical suggestions for you to use in protecting academic learning time. While instituting such suggestions takes readiness and commitment on the part of your staff, it also takes persuasion, convincing, and initiative on the part of administrators to unify staff on these matters. In the long run, one difference between good schools and great schools includes how well time is spent. Students depend on staff and administration to know what is in their best interest; they also depend on staff to practice effective methods.

Tips for Eliminating Interruptions and Extending Time-on-Task

- Schedule an inviolate "Academic, Uninterrupted Learning Time Block" for every day.
- Prohibit soliciting activities to raise money during school time.
- Schedule insurance payment pitches, photographs, and so on during lunch or after school.
- Review the time devoted to sports in relation to Academic Learning Time.
- Prohibit soliciting activities to raise money during school time.
- Replace track-and-field days with fitness programs.
- Schedule track-and-field days for after-school hours or on weekends.
- Prohibit or limit classroom interruptions by messengers, the PA system, visitors, pull-outs, and so on.
- Reduce the number of assemblies, rallies, rehearsals, and so on.
- Eliminate excessive film showings, both in classrooms and schoolwide.
- Conduct an "Academic Learning Time" audit.
- Use support staff or volunteers (not teachers) to take care of attendance, messages, and so on.
- Eliminate libraries closed for inventory and so on during school hours.
- Eliminate pull-out programs.
- Streamline routine logistics of tardiness and attendance.
- Delimit emergency personal phone calls, intercom calls, and so on.
- Reduce early dismissals, both official and unofficial ones.

- Reduce the number of times students change rooms and subjects.
- Eliminate the number of needless field trips.

The above list appears simple and practical, but its power lies in how well the suggestions can be instituted and maintained. The fact is (and get out your calculator for this one) that, by increasing time-on-task only three minutes per period per day, teachers and schools have dramatically increased achievement, with the qualification that this additional time is truly used substantively. Never underestimate how potent excellent teaching is: Just a few more minutes a day with uninterrupted, effective teaching, and your students will gain far more than from any one "flash-in-the-pan" new trend.

One elephant-sized difficulty an administrator will have in changing some of the above time-wasters is opposition from staff, if the practices are already in place. If this is the case, administrators will surely have to have their "ducks in order." In-service, consensus building, persistence, diplomacy, and effective communication will have to take high priority among administrative skills and practice. The case for eliminating or reducing the above time-wasters has been argued over and over again, and the outcome usually always translates to getting rid of them, but, obviously, an administrator will have to move cautiously if staff has an investment in these practices. This is no excuse, however, for not beginning to focus on ways to extend academic learning time. It may just take longer to finally achieve it in some schools. Schools that do show gains in student achievement, attendance, motivation, and self-discipline also display wise and productive use of time on both classroom and schoolwide bases.

A. *Academic Learning Time Audit*

Many administrators collect baseline data on their school's percentage of time-on-task by conducting "time-on-task" audits. There are many forms and formats, and several types should be used. One simple method that works for individual classrooms and that also can be used to arrive at a schoolwide percentage is illustrated in Figure 2.1. It requires the observer to identify the number of off-task behaviors coded over a defined period of time. At the end of the period, such as 45 minutes, the observer can calculate the percentage of "time-on-taskness" for that class during that period. Furthermore, in the form illustrated in Figure 2.1, specific students can also be coded for their off-task behaviors. This assists the teacher in diagnosing and modifying specific student behavior. To arrive at a school building percentage, an administrator can collect a random sample of individual classroom scores and then average them out.

B. *Absenteeism and Tardiness*

If students are losing academic learning time because of high rates of absenteeism and tardiness, then it goes without saying that achievement suffers. Some schools have a major problem with absenteeism and tardiness, and this problem is not limited to urban, inner-city schools. Often, suburban "middle-class" schools also exhibit lower-than-desirable attendance percentages, and the longer this condition remains unfixed, the more difficult it is to remedy. Unless all students are in attendance, the best curriculum is worthless and the most skilled teaching is in vain. Responsible attendance patterns provide students with heightened achievement, continuity of program, and citizenship development.

Attendance policies and procedures must be reviewed and possibly revised periodically, with the involvement of staff. This calls for alertness on the part of administrators to areas of need and an openness to shared decision making. Staff are in the best positions to know the patterns of absenteeism and tardiness, and their contribution to solving them is invaluable. But their hands are tied if the administrative procedures and expectations are unclear and lack clout. Your administrative actions can mean a real difference in lowering absenteeism and tardiness. The following checklist of indicators is intended to give you specific areas to be aware of and address in solving the problem of absenteeism. Again, if staff has a significant part in formulating

Room: <u>16</u>   Date: <u>September 22</u>   Time: <u>from 8:30 to 9:15</u>

Directions:

1. Every five minutes, do a "sweep," that is, "eyeball" each student in the room, and place a tally mark in the student box if the student is *off-task*.

After the first sweep, wait until the next five-minute interval and repeat the process. Continue this procedure until your observation time (e.g., 45 minutes) is up.

2. When your observation time block is completed:
    (a) count the total number of tally marks;
    (b) record this total on the "Total" line;
    (c) divide the total of off-task behaviors by the number of sweeps conducted;
    (d) divide that number by the number of students present;
    (e) subtract that answer from 100 for the percentage of "on-task" during your observation period.

EXAMPLE

<u>41</u>	Total number of tally marks

III		HHT	I	
II	II	HHT		III
II		IIII	I	
II	III		I	HHT II

<u> 9 </u> Number of sweeps
<u> 20 </u> Number of students present
<u>77%</u> Percentage of on-task students

Calculations:

(a) 41 tally marks ÷ 9 sweeps = 4.6 average
(b) 4.6 ÷ 20 students = 23%
(c) 100 − 23 = 77% on-task

Note: For a "regular" class under "regular" conditions, an "average" of 85% is considered good. (Some days would be lower, and other days higher. It's a good idea to take audits of the same class several times during a four to five week period, then average out the scores.)

Figure 2.1. Sample Academic Learning Time Observation Audit

and carrying out attendance procedures, your problem is more than solved.

Attendance Indicators Checklist

- An up-to-date attendance procedure and policy are in force.
- Standardized attendance-taking procedures are in use by all staff.
- A clearly defined system of excusing absences is in the handbook.
- An effective appeals process has been formulated and is in operation.
- Attendance policy and procedures are widely publicized among students and parents.
- Timely intervention for chronic absentees is in operation.
- Speedy follow-up on truants is effectively systematized.
- In-service of teachers in attendance procedures is up to date.
- An effective rewards-incentive system for attendance is in practice.
- Recognition for exemplary attendance is part of the reward system.

2.2 Designing Flexible Grouping Patterns of Staff and Students

Despite all the rhetoric of "reform" and "restructuring" and "success for all," very few schools have actually changed the outmoded structures of the "graded school" and "tracking." Until these structures are changed, not much will really change for students. This is not to imply that educators are uncaring, but it does imply that good, well-meaning educators appear locked into school organization structures that contradict best-practice research. We now know that there are more effective ways to organize schools and classrooms than continuing the graded school and the ability-grouping patterns that are in place in 99% of all U.S. schools. Most arguments in favor of continuing tracking and graded schools come from teachers and administrators who know the extreme difficulty of teaching classes with a wide range of ability. Another aspect concerns the difficulty most practicing educators have in conceiving of alternative, workable solutions. These concerns must be addressed. The teacher's ability to manage a widely diverse group of students is paramount to the students' success. There are solutions to this real problem, and the following models are ways to organize students and staff on a schoolwide and classroom basis.

A. *Paired Block Time and Organization of Staff at the Elementary Level*

Paired (or Parallel) Block Time scheduling is an excellent, alternative approach to organizing time and staff that permits uninterrupted small group instruction for all students every day. It entails regrouping students and staff in ways that are different than the traditional 1:25 ratio of teachers to students. Benefits of this model include

(a) reducing the teacher-pupil ratio (e.g., 1:14) for parts of the day, in particular for the basic skills or high-priority subjects;
(b) eliminating pull-outs;
(c) increasing teacher time for direct instruction in basic skills;
(d) integrating (rather than intruding) support services into the pupils' academic life;
(e) avoiding low self-image of remedial students by not singling them out for services;
(f) assisting in smoother mainstreaming of students from special education classes;
(g) providing alternatives for staff members' assignments;
(h) eliminating ability "tracking" in favor of flexible, heterogeneous skills grouping; and
(i) increasing teacher collaboration and team planning for student success.

Paired Block Time scheduling is illustrated in Figure 2.2. Note that the entire day is segmented into time blocks that fit

Scheduling and Configuring Schools 31

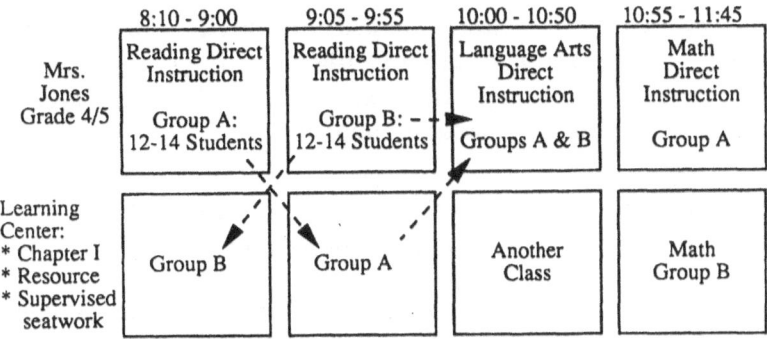

Figure 2.2. Paired Block Scheduling

the allotment of time for curricular subjects, movement of students to different locations, and arrangement of teachers to accommodate student grouping needs rather than having students accommodate teachers' unique scheduling assignments.

As an example of the model illustrated in Figure 2.2, each teacher would be assigned two reading groups or math groups, a "homeroom" period, science, and social studies. During the allotted time for reading, for example, while one reading group is being instructed by the classroom teacher (usually 12-14 students), the other group has moved to the center for enrichment, supervised seat work, or to special services, such as Chapter 1, speech, or band. There is no "seat work;" that is, "down time." After the period is over, the groups reverse; the center/special service groups go to their reading class, and the reading class group goes to the center or to special support services. The "center" can be any area capable of receiving students for supervised learning activities: the cafeteria, library, hallway, media center, empty classrooms, and so on.

This model virtually eliminates time-filler seat work, because the teacher is able to spend the entire period in active, intense instruction with all of the students in that particular group. Of course, the support teachers must be scheduled to receive the special students at the designated times during which the classroom teachers are teaching reading or math. After the small group, direct instruction in reading and math, students are recombined for further language arts work in handwriting and other activities or for PE, music, computers, and so on. Note that students are flexibly grouped; that is, they may be in a lower reading group but also in a higher math group. Tracking is not allowed. (For a further explanation of how this type of model works, refer to Canady, 1990.)

B. *Cooperative Learning Grouping: An Alternative to Tracking at the Middle and High School Levels*

Grouping students for success and productive time-on-task requires ingenuity, an awareness of the potential negative effects of tracking, and a genuine desire to use proven, albeit nonconventional, strategies in classroom teaching. One model that has captured national attention (but not widespread implementation, especially at the secondary level) is cooperative learning. The research supporting this model has more than proven itself for raising student achievement, improving student social skills, enhancing positive multicultural diversity and appreciation, and strengthening student cooperation and collaboration. (If you are interested in researching this topic, prominent names in this field include S. Kagan, Johnson and Johnson, and R. Slavin.)

In the basic cooperative learning model, students are heterogeneously mixed in small (three to five) learning groups within the classroom. The teacher provides each group with learning goals, and students interact interdependently, relying on and assisting each other for active participation and cooperation in achieving group learning goals. Peer teaching and learning, a safe psychological environment, and the reduction of threatening competition and frustration characterize this model. It is, however, more complex teaching than that using the standard lesson design and delivery, and it requires staff development for teachers and for administrators. One way to successfully initiate the program is to interest and capitalize upon those teachers who are open to change and innovation. Then arrange for an appealing staff development session introducing these teachers to the model, including its effects and results.

Teachers need and deserve good staff development in this model, including the accompanying coaching and feedback by their supervisors (or trained peers) for "surefire" implementation. Administrators also need the same, with additional in-service in the areas of coaching and formative supervision. So far, elementary teachers and administrators by far have been the most numerous consumers and users of this excellent instructional model.

If you are a secondary administrator, you have a particularly monumental challenge: Secondary teachers tend to be cemented in the use of lecture and other teacher-dominated instructional methods. Because secondary teachers generally view themselves as "subject matter specialists," they usually tend to deemphasize instructional delivery expertise and student-centered approaches in favor of amassing content knowledge. Instruction in secondary schools seems to be based on the belief that students have to be grouped homogeneously. This translates to whole group, competitive instruction; lecturing as the dominant form of delivery; common assignments and due dates; and one set of grading standards.

Few secondary teachers have had extensive experiences attempting to teach heterogeneous groups at the secondary level. They appear to believe that two or three distinctly different groups mixed together cannot possibly receive the high quality of instruction that they now give to high-ability students. The fact is that there are ways to effectively teach all students in a heterogeneously grouped class. But it does require an attitude shift (i.e., "paradigm" shift?) in terms of the way to do it. Cooperative learning is one significant, workable approach. If you are interested in having your school break from the conventional mold, begin by identifying a few highly motivated teachers who are willing to innovate. Allocate the funds for them to receive staff development. Promote and reinforce them. Plan out a three- to five-year program in which you will incrementally provide in-service in cooperative learning to all willing and able staff. Market your school as a "cooperative learning" one. You will see student achievement and attitude dramatically improve if the program is seriously implemented and time is allowed for the program to mature. The list below identifies steps administrators may take to launch a cooperative learning approach in schools.

- Allocate funds for three to five (or more, if possible) teachers to receive staff development in cooperative learning.
- Identify three to five (or more, if possible) willing and enthusiastic teachers who are motivated and willing to try this teaching model.
- Arrange for these teachers to read about and hear expert, dynamic speakers on cooperative learning.
- Send them to (or have the trainers come in for) cooperative learning training.
- Support their enthusiasm; listen to their problems; promote their efforts.
- Advertise the teachers' in-service program in the district newsletter.
- Develop a three- to five-year staff development plan and time line for cooperative learning training and implementation. (For "action planning," see Chapter 1.)
- Market your school as a "Cooperative Learning School." (For marketing suggestions, refer to Chapter 1.)
- Keep track of student progress in the cooperative learning classrooms. (Include the teachers in your plans.)
- Keep the district office informed of the project and invite them to visit the classrooms.
- Ask the district research or testing coordinator to design an evaluation system that collects student progress information in the cooperative learning classrooms. (Again, include the teachers in the plan.)
- Advertise among parents and community the cooperative learning model and student progress.
- Add more teachers to the pool of cooperative learning teachers by gradually inviting more to join.
- Plan for a tiered model of staff development to emerge: those who are experienced and those who are beginners. (Eventually, the experienced teachers can train the newcomers.)

While cooperative learning models can be used in all subjects at every grade level, it is not desirable that it be used exclusively (as are the "lecture" and "discussion" models). Rather, it should be viewed as another highly effective model to add to a teacher's repertoire of instructional tools.

This model is especially suited to schools (such as middle schools) whose philosophy touts "cooperation and collaboration" and "multidisciplinary teaching." Its response to multicultural diversity and to various learning styles is especially powerful. Its greatest contribution is to improved student achievement, time-on-task, and student motivation. Social studies teachers who emphasize experiential and hands-on approaches in teaching democratic principles of government and citizenship may be especially drawn to this model, for it puts into classroom practice a "citizens' approach to teaching and learning."

c. Break From the Exclusive Use of the "5 × 45"-Minute Daily Schedule (or Others Like it)

Although attempts at modular scheduling have pretty much disappeared over the past 20 years, the need for larger blocks of time still remains for multidisciplinary teaching and learning groupings. Instead of a constant fare of five 45-minute periods per day, why not extend some classes, such as English, social studies, mathematics, and foreign language, to a 135-minute laboratory weekly or once every two weeks? This arrangement allows interdisciplinary teaching, learning, and in-depth treatment of content. It also encourages prioritization of curriculum objectives.

2.3 Accessing Special Programs and Services for Widely Diverse Students

Another area of focus on time and personnel is in integrating special programs for your widely diverse student body. In addition to the demographic makeup of your school with respect to race, ethnicity, and socioeconomic status, all of your students have a variety of learning needs and interests. Special education, Chapter 1, gifted, honors, advanced placement, and other programs speak to the scope and breadth of academic and social needs of students. In the beginning of public school history, the handicapped, racial minorities, and other "special" students were segregated from the mainstream of school life. As time passed, educators attempted to respond to diversity by designing a uniform framework of time scheduling and groupings of teaching personnel. This uniform framework was amazingly similar in districts across the country, that is, a ratio of about 1:25, pull-outs for special programs, segregation of special education students, and so on. Slowly, over the years, integration of all students into the mainstream has been promoted and, in some schools, has succeeded. But the stigma of special students who don't fit the norm (whatever the "norm" may be; that is, "white" or "normal" or "nonhandicapped" or "keeping up to grade level" and so on) remains in the majority of schools. This has stained the hoped-for success that every student deserves to experience.

Teachers who manage large numbers of highly diverse students have a monumental challenge and deserve all the managerial support possible. Some schools in the country are responding to this challenge by innovating with new types of scheduling and teaching models. They are working toward eliminating "pull-out" models of special service programs for students and also minimizing the rigid segregation of teachers and students into strictly "regular" or "special." While federal and state categorical compliance issues must be followed for licensure and special programs, there is still room for creative, nonconventional groupings of "special" and "regular" students and teachers that maximize student outcomes and teacher performance. These models are labeled with a variety of names, such as "Merge," "Consultative," or "Team."

A. *Team Approach to Assisting Diverse or At-Risk Students*

Elementary and secondary student assistance teams of professionals constitute one type of model. On the team may be an administrator, school nurse, psychologist, and several teachers as well as any other professional needed for the case. The team meets formally in accordance with a predetermined schedule. Through the team approach, all the professionals can support

Scheduling and Configuring Schools 37

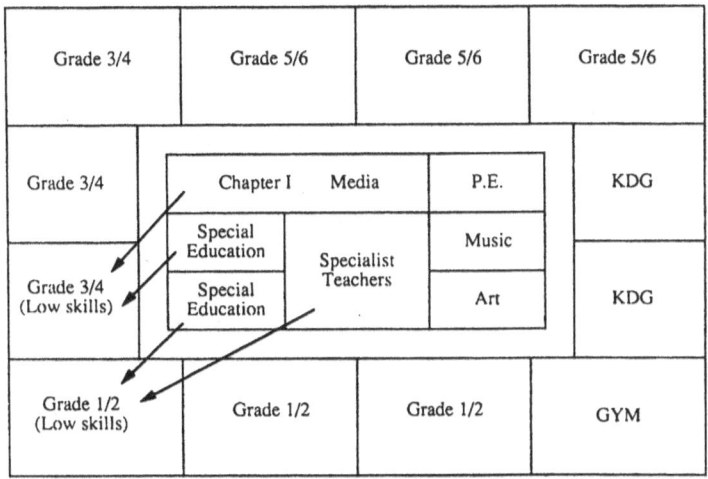

Figure 2.3. Example of Split Grade or Continuous Progress

the student's teacher or teachers in a variety of ways. They can initiate changes in the student's schedule and provide resources and ongoing problem solving. Scheduling meetings to apply interventions and to debrief solutions to a particular case are part of the model. This removes the isolation and single-perspective approach so prevalent in the traditional model in which the individual classroom teacher is pretty much "on her own" in solving problems. (For additional information on the team approach, refer to Ogden and Germinario, 1988.)

B. *Split-Grade Model or Continuous Progress Model*

The Split-Grade (or "Continuous Progress") Model is a variation of the "Paired Block Model" at the elementary level described earlier in the chapter. In the Split-Grade Model, students in all grades and classrooms are grouped with other students within one grade span of their own, either "up" or "down." This arrangement places students together who are at similar skill levels. Each teacher has this combination-class for most of the day, at least during the block of time for basic skills.

Figure 2.3 illustrates this split-grade arrangement. This model can also be viewed as a "continuous progress" one, for it allows students to work at their respective instructional levels and move to the next level when ready to do so. Students are evaluated every three to four weeks and regrouped. This maintains integrity of skills grouping and avoids tracking. The special teachers move to the low-skills groups and the students are not pulled out in this model.

The merits of this model include

(a) integrating students who share common learning needs,
(b) avoiding "tracking" or homogeneous ability grouping,
(c) assisting teachers in managing instruction by reducing the wide span of learning needs within a typical conventional grade,
(d) eliminating the pull-out program,
(e) giving teachers the opportunity to plan together and team their expertise in problem solving and individual learning plans for students, and
(f) allowing students to move forward when ready.

By having both "average" third and "lower" fourth graders, for example, who are on a similar math or reading level, teachers are able to focus more intense instruction on fewer groups within one instructional setting, thus increasing teacher-pupil interaction. In this model, teachers who have the lower-achieving students also have the special education/resource teachers in their classroom at a designated time, and they team teach the class. This is not only in alignment with compliance regulations for categorical programs, such as Chapter 1, it also eliminates pulling out students.

Students in this Split-Grade or Continuous Progress Model are not together all day but rejoin their respective grade peers for such subjects as social studies and science/health. Also, it is important that the special teachers be available at specific times during the day, which accommodates the movement of students. This avoids the singling out of students for special services as well as reducing the regular teachers' large number of instructional levels. Also, during the team planning period of

TABLE 2.1 Multiage Model

Ages 5-7	Ages 7-9	Ages 9-11	Ages 11-13
Staff Team	Staff Team	Staff Team	Staff Team
3-4 Teachers (interdisciplinary)	3-4 Teachers (interdisciplinary)	3-4 Teachers (interdisciplinary)	3-4 Teachers (interdisciplinary)
120 Students	120 Students	120 Students	120 Students
1-2 Paraprofessionals	1-2 Paraprofessionals	1-2 Paraprofessionals	1-2 Paraprofessionals
Special Services Core	Special Services Core	Special Services Core	Special Services Core

the grade 3/4 teachers, for example, students take their music, PE, and art classes.

c. Multiage Grouping

Another variation of the Split-Grade Model for the elementary school is the Multiage Model. This format uses chronological age as its organizing factor and divides the entire elementary school into age groupings. The entire school is arranged into four age categories: (a) ages 5-7, (b) ages 7-9, (c) ages 9-11, and (d) ages 11-13. This arrangement allows at-risk and other special students to be mixed into homogeneous groups as well as into appropriate instructional levels for the teacher. It also allows flexible skill grouping within each of the respective age groups. Additionally, each group may be assigned the services of special resource teachers/consultants whose responsibilities would be to serve that group exclusively. Table 2.1 illustrates the Multiage school arrangement.

Note also in the table that flexibility in staffing is possible; that is, instead of four teachers for 120 students, perhaps three with a paraprofessional would work out very well. This model would also work well if specialists and resource teachers went into classrooms to team teach rather than pulling out students from their regular classes. Or this model could be mixed with the Paired Block Model or the Split-Grade Model in which students are not pulled out for special services but their special services are integrated within the regular day's curriculum and program.

2.4 Evaluating Administrative Duties in Organizing Schools for Achievement

Identifying administrative duties with respect to the organization of time, staff, and students for maximum achievement requires targeting the desired outcomes and the administrative actions that are the means to attain them. The following evaluation form is not exhaustive or inclusive, nor is it "divinely inspired." It is, however, a set of statements that can be used to assess what needs to be done to enhance time and personnel for school improvement. You are encouraged to evaluate yourself by completing the form in Table 2.2 ("low-risk" action). High risk takers may want to give it to staff to gain a broader perspective. At any rate, it addresses salient points for maximizing time and personnel.

2.5 Summary

Of all the considerations on the table for improving student achievement, the organization of time, staff, and students is of prime importance. While other factors may have more visibility and staff support, these factors are so weighty and so mighty that most other school improvement techniques and trends will be short-lived and shallow without them. Furthermore, organization of time and staff to accommodate student achievement requires administrators to be tenacious and creative in both management and leadership. Improvement in these areas will far surpass the effects of other school improvement efforts.

TABLE 2.2 Organizing Time and Students for Increasing Achievement

(Check the boxes that apply to your school)

Scheduling Time
- ☐ An audit of Time-On-Task has been conducted for individual classrooms and on a schoolwide basis.
- ☐ Interruptions in the teaching/learning process are prohibited.
- ☐ Public address announcements and intercom messages are strictly reduced to a minimum.
- ☐ Staff has participated in Academic Learning Time in-service.
- ☐ Noninstructional activities performed by teachers (e.g., attendance) have been streamlined and minimized.
- ☐ A system of improving attendance and punctuality has been instituted.
- ☐ Transitions between and within classes have been reviewed and reduced.
- ☐ Nonprofessional staff or volunteers assist in the noninstructional aspects of attendance, delivering messages, and so on.

Groupings of Staff and Students

Elementary schools:
- ☐ The entire school is organized around flexible skills groupings for a variety of subjects.
- ☐ Teachers do not have more than two skills groups to work with in one period.
- ☐ Students are not pulled out of class for special programs.
- ☐ Teachers have received staff development in skills grouping and/or cooperative learning.
- ☐ Teachers are using cooperative learning skillfully and appropriately.
- ☐ Special education and resource teachers' assignments work in conjunction with regular education teachers.
- ☐ Teachers have team planning time for instructional and interdisciplinary planning.
- ☐ The entire facility has been carefully investigated for extra space for alternative grouping needs.
- ☐ Basic skills subjects are delivered to a smaller number of students than in other subjects.

(continued)

TABLE 2.2 (continued)

Secondary schools:

- ❑ Ability grouping (tracking) is not in practice.
- ❑ Teachers have team planning time in their schedules for interdisciplinary instruction.
- ❑ Some blocks of time during the week are extended for some subjects (e.g., "laboratories" and so on).
- ❑ Absenteeism and tardiness are well controlled.
- ❑ Teachers have received effective in-service in flexible skills grouping and/or cooperative learning.
- ❑ Athletes, music students, and other performance students are not pulled out of instruction in their other subjects.
- ❑ Teachers differentiate their instruction and assignments to fit the diversity within each of the classes.
- ❑ Grading philosophy and practice are in alignment with "success for every student."
- ❑ Cooperative learning is being used in classrooms successfully.

References

Canady, R. L. (1988). A cure for fragmented schedules in elementary schools. *Educational Leadership, 46,* 65-67.

Canady, R. L. (1990). A better way to organize a school. *Principal, 1,* 34-36.

Cuban, L. (1989). The "at-risk" label and the problem of urban school reform. *Phi Delta Kappan, 45,* 780-801.

Good, T. L., & Brophy, J. E. (1987). *Looking in classrooms.* New York: Harper & Row.

Ogden, E. H., & Germinario, V. (1988). *The at-risk student.* Lancaster, PA: Technomic.

Slavin, R. E. (1990). Achievement effects of ability grouping in secondary school: A best-evidence synthesis. *Review of Educational Research, 60*(3), 471-499.

3

Providing Sound Ancillary Services for Effective Schools

Schools are only as good as their communities think they are. Community perceptions of schools are vital aspects of their effectiveness. Community perceptions of schools are often built upon experiences and interactions with ancillary services or staff—the look and appearance of grounds or buildings and dealings with bus drivers, custodians, food service workers, maintenance workers, and so on. Such perceptions could be positive or negative, depending upon the nature of the experience.

Neither satisfaction nor educational effectiveness occur in a vacuum. Unquestionably, instruction has to be developed to produce optimal learning, but the school administrator's responsibility does not end there. Students have to be transported to school, meals have to be provided while students are there, and office procedures have to efficiently accommodate the needs of clients. The better you develop and implement quality ancillary services and programs, the better you are able to advance educational success.

3.1 Ancillary Services Defined

Ancillary services comprise any activity or resource use that is subordinate and helpful to the delivery of instructional services. Instructional quality in large part is dependent upon the extent and nature of ancillary services. Without efficiency in transportation, food service, office and risk management, and enterprise operations, the quality of a school can be seriously limited or even impaired. As one wizened school administrator once lamented, "It's important to get good learning in a school, but first you have to run the place." "Running the place" in a way to "get good learning" is what this chapter is all about.

3.2 Ancillary Services: Scope of Support and Assistance

The purpose of this chapter is to set the framework for school administrators who are interested in providing appropriate ancillary services in support of an effective educational program. To do this, six topics in ancillary services will be discussed. The first deals with the administrative responsibilities in risk management; the second, with guidelines for sound office management. The third topic describes key elements in the operation of student transportation services, and the fourth topic outlines precepts of efficient school food services. The fifth topic addresses the operation of "enterprise," or revenue-producing operations. The sixth and final topic grapples with the issue of privatization, or external contracting for services.

3.3 Risk Management

Risk simply means exposure to possible harm, injury, or loss. Risk also includes an element of chance. Chances are that your school will not suffer much loss but the rare occurrence that it might calls for action on your part. The challenge is to minimize the risks involved in operating a school while holding a reasonable line on costs.

A. *Trends in Risk Exposure*

Several factors have increased the risk exposure of schools and school administrators. Courts have ruled that public institutions are no longer immune to lawsuits. Violence has increased in schools. Environmental hazards like lead, asbestos, and even radioactive contamination have plagued all organizations. Settlements and awards in tort liability suits have reached staggering levels in many cases. A great deal of money is at risk in school operations. Insurance companies have become less enthusiastic about insuring schools, while at the same time the need for comprehensive risk management couldn't be greater.

B. *Options for Administrative Action*

Choices are available for you in administering a sound risk management program. The last choice you may want to make is to purchase insurance. Some prior choices include avoidance, assumption, reduction, and transfer of risk in your school operations.

Risk avoidance. Schools have found that the cheapest way to handle risk is to avoid it altogether. For example, after huge losses and expense, schools have generally eliminated high-risk programs and operations. Few, if any, trampolines remain in schools. Junior rodeos have gone the way of Main Street shootouts in the western states. Hazardous equipment, sometimes called attractive nuisance, has been reconfigured or redesigned for greater safety. These are ways in which schools have avoided risk. You probably exercise considerable discretion in determining the nature of the program of activities at your school. For example, if a class wanted to go on a field trip to the neighborhood fire station, you'd probably allow it. On the other hand, if a class wanted to go to the Grand Canyon to learn hang gliding, you'd be foolish to permit it. Probability of hazard and severity of injury are two factors to mix in with common sense in risk avoidance.

Risk assumption. Some risks are worth taking. For example, if you have school personnel residing on school sites or electronic alarms in schools, as is common in many communities, you might not insure against all forms of vandalism. The risk is small under such circumstances. Or if you have smoke detectors and automatic fire sprinklers in your classrooms, you have assumed part of the risk of fire, which will save you a bundle in insurance premiums. Of course, the best place to assume risk and control insurance cost is in the *design* of facilities. Most of the risk you might assume should be in cases of small risk and insignificant cost.

Risk reduction. Reducing risk is another way to manage potential loss. Measures you take in school planning and operations can make a huge difference. For example, one school district, after losing all of its buses in a fire, learned the hard way about dispersion of vehicles. Another school averted tragedy in a tornado by having prepared and executing an excellent catastrophe plan. Factors around your school to reduce risk can be pointed out to you by safety inspectors, fire marshals, and insurance loss control consultants.

Risk transfer. Transferring risk to someone else, or to another organization, is another option for you to consider. One school district, after suffering several employee accidents that caused their workers' compensation premium to triple, began contracting for maintenance services with expert external firms. If you restrict your staff from unsafe activities, and use other means to get certain work accomplished, risk can be shifted. For example, instead of asking your custodian to climb up the tall tree in front of your school to remove a broken limb, it's more advisable to call in an expert tree service. With their sophisticated equipment and highly trained and experienced personnel, any risk remaining is transferred to them. Risk transfer is one of the advantages of privatization of certain services.

Last choice: Purchase insurance. Insurance against loss should be bought when risk can't be avoided, assumed, reduced, or transferred. Types of risk insurance (excluding employee benefits) for schools include workers compensation, property and casualty, catastrophe, general liability, fidelity bonding, errors and omissions, product liability, and automobile coverage. Getting good advice in purchasing insurance is difficult at best and often nearly impossible. Most advice is provided by providers, or sales people, of insurance and is obviously not without bias. Professional literature does provide a modicum of help along these lines (Jordan et al., 1987; Randall, 1986).

3.4 Office Management

Managing the office sounds easy. It isn't. You have many things to deal with in a busy school office, including records and reports, equipment and materials, and office personnel. A well-organized office contributes to the whole school's efficiency and quality of service.

A. Records and Reports

School policies, state regulations, and federal law all affect the nature, use, and handling of school records and reports. Every effort must be made to safeguard and protect records and confidential information, to eliminate duplication in record keeping, to maximize computerization of data bases (see Chapter 7), to control access to records, and to comply with appropriate principles of record handling in schools. The "paper shuffle" constantly pesters busy administrators. Given good organization and planning, records can be handled easily and efficiently. The following is a suggested list of 10 priority areas in handling student records:

1. minimum pupil data maintained by schools,
2. student or parent requests for inspection of records,
3. notification of students and parents about destruction of records,
4. access to student records and confidentiality rights,
5. notification and requests for student records by third parties,
6. consent for release of student records,
7. care and safekeeping of student records,
8. release of information to student's new school,
9. documentation of actions taken with student records, and
10. retention and archiving of student information.

B. *Office Organization*

A good test of the administrator's office organization is how well the office operates in his or her absence. Moreover, how well the office serves the educational mission of the school is another test of quality. Factors to evaluate in office organization are delineated in the list that follows:

1. Policies and procedures are defined, cataloged, disseminated, and accessible.
2. Office procedures, including forms, are documented in operations manual.
3. Files are systematically arranged, retrievable, and secure from fire or loss.
4. Staff development and training are planned and provided for office personnel.
5. Daily, weekly, and monthly tasks are defined, listed, and monitored.

Providing Sound Ancillary Services

6. Job descriptions are established for all office and administrative positions.
7. A schedule of office routines is established, posted, and flexible.
8. The access procedure for office services is established and disseminated.
9. Size and configuration of office are congruent with proper work conditions.
10. Work and interpersonal climate is pleasant, positive, and collaborative.
11. Equipment, materials, and time-saving tools are adequate and suitable.
12. Supervision is based upon growth-producing evaluation and direction.

Given healthy office organization and appropriate records practices, office management contributes to the enhancement of educational opportunity in your school.

3.5 Transportation

An early job description for a school bus driver established many conditions for school transportation services that continue to the present day, as shown in the list of school bus driver rules below.

The driver will:

1. Furnish a safe, strong team with proper harness.
2. Refrain from fast driving and racing other teams.
3. Maintain order among students to and from school.
4. Refrain from use of profanity in addressing team or students.
5. Refrain from use of tobacco in presence of students.
6. Shall wait 3 minutes for a child, and blow a loud whistle. (Bronson School, Woodbury County, Iowa)

Managing transportation services hasn't changed much in terms of the issues involved, such as safety, operation requirements, and pupil behavior management. Today's school administrator, however, finds many complex issues and problems to deal with in obtaining a quality transportation system.

School bus transportation is perhaps the safest form of motor vehicle transportation. About 22 million school children are transported more than 3.3 billion miles annually in the United States. Parents deserve to have high confidence in school transportation systems, and getting that confidence is your administrative challenge.

A. *Transportation Policies*

Any good transportation system has rational, well-thought-out principles and values defined in policy. Key policy issues are listed below:

(a) eligibility for transportation services;
(b) mode of service and range of services provided;
(c) route planning and establishment guidelines;
(d) safety standards and requirements, including training of staff;
(e) equipment procurement rules and specifications;
(f) inspection and maintenance of transportation equipment;
(g) bus driver duties and responsibilities;
(h) bus driver qualifications, selection, and employment conditions;
(i) routing and scheduling methods, including the way distances are measured;
(j) transportation for extracurricular and nonschool activities;
(k) fiscal management guidelines including expense reimbursement, if any;
(l) alternative modes of transportation in special circumstances;
(m) plans and procedures for evaluation of transportation staff and services;

(n) pupil behavior requirements and regulations; and
(o) administrative responsibilities.

B. *Administrative Duties*

School transportation is a complex enterprise requiring complex administrative tasks and attention. You may have to assume many of the responsibilities delineated below, depending upon the size and qualifications of your district and staff.

Policy Ramifications

Sound transportation services will be based upon sound policy. Policy must be developed with the participation of all parties involved in the delivery of services and adopted by the governing board to "institutionalize" the rules and practices that are acceptable. In the absence of comprehensive policy, confusion and inefficiencies will result. Policy will need to be translated into administrative and operational procedures, and you will be expected to implement policies. Policy determination is a board governance function; carrying out policies is an administrative function.

Operational Particulars

To operate the transportation system, you'll need to perform many of the following tasks:

Determine the eligibility of passengers.
Enforce standards of behavior.
Set standard mileage limitations.
Define pickup locations and stops.
Design and define efficient routes.
Determine conditions for suspension of service.
Enforce safety rules and considerations.
Provide for a comprehensive maintenance system.
Recommend specifications for equipment purchase.
Monitor condition of bus fleet.

Inform community of needs and performance results.
Schedule and supervise personnel.

Driver Supervision

There is little question that the school bus driver is one of the most important members of the school district team, but recent trends point out increasing difficulties in securing qualified personnel. Driver qualifications are stringent, and rightfully so when safety factors are considered. Driver qualifications must be carefully defined, and selection procedures must assure that physical, ethical, operational, and behavioral requirements are properly met.

All drivers of buses can benefit from operative staff development programs. Safety, efficiency, driving skill, student behavior management, preventative maintenance, conservation of resources, and management duties can be enhanced with well-planned training programs. In addition, emergency procedures must be strengthened and perfected by the staff development program.

Vehicle Maintenance

Equipment failure can jeopardize your transportation system if maintenance isn't well planned and executed. Daily inspections must be required, and you should check occasionally to assure that they are being performed. Drivers should check under the hood, inside the bus, outside the bus, and all instruments prior to operations for the day. If maintenance is due, it needs to be provided on schedule.

Safety

There is nothing more important in school bus transportation system management that assuring safe and sound service. Your responsibility in providing a comprehensive safety program for buses must focus on equipment design and reliability, driver qualifications and training, student instruction on safe practices, comprehensive equipment maintenance, and public credibility.

Public demands for transportation systems will continue to increase in the future as they have in the past. Your job is to keep abreast of the needs and requirements of a modern, effective system of transportation and to be sure your students are served with the best program possible.

3.6 Food Services

There are two major responsibilities in administering your food service program: providing nutritionally adequate meals in a cost-effective manner, and complying with all state and federal laws and regulations. Neither is easy to do, yet, in this country, more than 4 billion meals are served in schools annually.

Ironically, federal school meal programs began originally because of national security concerns. Excessive numbers of draftees failed to meet physical admission standards for military service during World War II, resulting in Congress passing the School Lunch Act in 1946. Schools began serving meals in accordance with federal regulations and continue to do so today. Of course, the regulations have multiplied and changed over time, making your job of administering the program more complex.

A. *Administrative Responsibilities*

As an administrator, you are responsible for everything that goes on (and sometimes for things that don't go on) at your school. In the area of food services, your supervisory duties and obligations should be limited only to the priority issues involved. These responsibilities include meal planning and delivery, facilities support, and meal counting and claiming.

Meal Planning

Of course, most administrators delegate this responsibility to qualified subordinates, but supervisors worth their salt know

TABLE 3.1 School Lunch Program Required Meal Components

Food group	Ages 3-8	Age 9 or Over
Meat or meat alternate	1.5 oz	2.0 oz
Vegetable or fruit (2 servings)	1/2 cup each	3/4 cup each
Bread or Bread alternate	1 slice or equivalent	1 slice or equivalent
Fluid whole or > 2% fat milk	8 fl. oz	8 fl. oz

TABLE 3.2 School Breakfast Required Meal Components

Food Group	All Ages
Fluid whole or > 2% fat milk	1 serving
Vegetable or fruit	1 serving
Bread or bread alternate or Meat or meat alternate	2 servings (any combination)

how to tell whether the delegation is working satisfactorily. Such working knowledge is very useful, because failure to provide appropriate elements in meals results in the possible loss of federal reimbursement for costs of those meals. In 1991, about $.75 per eligible meal was provided to local schools from the federal government for each lunch served. Even in small schools, that can amount to a lot of money.

Meal Pattern Requirements

Eligible meals comprise the five elements shown in both Tables 3.1 and 3.2.

Meal Configuration

To reduce food waste, federal rules, called OVS (offer versus serve), require that all five food items in the above exhibit must be offered (or made available) to all students to be reimbursable. Also, the serving size must equal or exceed quantities specified by the rules. No fewer than three of the five items offered must be taken, but the lunch must be priced as a unit, and students may take three, four, or all five items for the same price.

Variations are permitted for medical or special dietary needs; religious, ethnic, or economic needs; foreign meal patterns; and milk supply constraints. Planning menus in school requires special skill and care. It is very difficult to provide meals that are both acceptable for reimbursement and appealing to students. Meals that are not fully consumed do not deliver full nutritional value, and a successful food service program must adapt menu items accordingly.

Ironically, under current rules, a school lunch of a Taco salad, rice pudding, and milk would be reimbursable, while a lunch of oven-fried chicken, mashed potatoes, gelatin cubes, and milk would not be reimbursable. Your job is to assure that your lunch program is carefully supervised to continue qualification for reimbursement for all meals while delivering nutritional value as well.

Elements of an Acceptable Counting-Claiming System

One of the things that can strike a chill into the heart of administrators is notification that their lunch program, or a portion of it, is not entitled to reimbursement because of faulty administration. Unfortunately, such loss of revenue can come after the fact and too late to rectify. Most reimbursement claim rejection is due to failure to provide an acceptable counting and claiming system.

Federal reimbursement is provided for each meal that meets the National School Lunch/Breakfast Program requirements *and* is served to an eligible student. To obtain reimbursement, you have to count, record, and claim the number of meals actually served to students in various categories. The categories are of three types: paid, reduced price, and free. Free and reduced-price meals claimed for reimbursement must have adequate documentation in support of the claim. The six documentation requirements are provided in Table 3.3.

TABLE 3.3 Elements of an Acceptable Counting and Claiming System

Element	Description
Eligibility documentation	Current, approved application or list from food stamp or Aid to Families with Dependent Children (AFDC) agencies
Collection procedures	Collection of payment for meals without overt identification of students eligible for free or reduced-price meals
Meal counts	Point of service verification that a reimbursable or paid meal has been served to an eligible student
Records and reports	Accurate records of reimbursable meals reported in easily read format for consolidated monthly claims
Reimbursement claims	Submission of meal counts on daily, weekly, and monthly basis with categorical breakdowns by type
Internal controls	Audit checks and monitoring of program to assure accuracy in claims for reimbursement

School meal programs are big business. Administrators must employ skills in marketing, fiscal reporting, waste management, cost analysis, staffing, staff development, warehousing, procurement, distribution, and a host of other competencies. Food service problems arise from rising labor costs, food price increases, tougher nutritional standards, uneven cash flow, and unfair competition. Whether such programs stay under school supervision depends upon the skill and business savvy used by administrators. In a growing number of districts, commercial firms are taking over school food service operations with varying levels of success. You have a number of steps to take if you want to operate an effective food service program, as delineated in the list that follows:

Providing Sound Ancillary Services

1. Integrate food service with the school's educational program.
2. Clearly establish sound organizational management of food service program and personnel with decentralized (site-based) "line" responsibilities.
3. Create and implement pleasing environments for food service for healthy eating habits, manners, behavior, and decorum.
4. Improve and maintain food quality and presentation with expanded choices.
5. Control financial operations with sound accounting and cash management procedures.
6. Inspect and maintain equipment and supplies for efficiency, safekeeping, and preservation.

Educational program opportunities are plentiful in food service programs, but studies indicate little connection between the two. Instructional program components could include nutritional benefits and food selection, maintenance of proper diet, career opportunities in food service industries, socialization and proper dining behavior, health implications of sanitation and waste management, and multicultural dimensions of foods around the world. Your school would benefit immensely from proper use of the food service resources available to your educational program.

Knowledge and understanding of the national and state issues and aspects of school food service are helpful in decision making in your school. Food services, to be effective, demand the same attention as any other quality program under your supervision.

3.7 Enterprise Operations

Business operations in schools are nothing new. Commodities, services, and products have been sold in school settings for many years, usually for the purpose of supplementing or augmenting public support and financing. Enterprise operations are businesslike undertakings in schools that involve production of

TABLE 3.4 Typical Enterprise Operations in Schools

Program Sphere of Activity	Description of Operations
Community and adult schools	Evening or alternative courses and programs
Food service operations	Lunch and/or breakfast plus other food sales
Other schooling programs	Recreational, preschool, day care
Summer school programs	Credit courses and noncredit classes
Renting or leasing school buildings	To community organizations or groups
Special extracurricular programs	Swimming lessons, driver education, and so on
Vending operations	Pupil supplies, snacks, beverages, confections
Service provider activities	Data processing, clerical services, and so on
Advertising sales	On campuses and in school publications
User fees and service charges	Lockers, towels, optional services

goods or services for financial return, generally a profit. There are many such operations in schools that produce revenues, and examples are listed in Table 3.4. As a rule, most enterprise operations are revenue producing from fees, tuition, sales, or other income.

3.8 Expansion of Support

Schools have considerable opportunity to expand their resources beyond what is normally provided by taxation and the public sector. As the administrator in charge, you should explore the opportunities afforded your school in enterprise operations and consider augmenting your resources with such programs.

Offering some of the enterprise programs in your school not only produces income for your school but in many cases provides a needed service for your community. For example, one district found that their after-school program met a crying need for child care for working parents. Moreover, the program produced enough revenue beyond expenses to purchase many items of much-needed school equipment.

One superintendent in Phoenix, Arizona, created a private foundation in support of his school district, complete with a board of trustees and appropriate articles of incorporation. The foundation raised more than $100,000 in its first year of operation from contributions, fund-raising activities, and enterprise operations. Such experience is not uncommon. More and more schools are discovering the advantages of privately financed, nonprofit school foundations. Given the private sector advantages, foundations can significantly expand the fund-raising capacity of schools. Foundations provide an excellent vehicle for community involvement in schools and enable the schools to bond with alumni, parents, and community patrons. Funds from foundations can be used for a wide variety of school projects and improvements, including programs, equipment, facilities, and student activities.

3.9 Privatization

In the quest for improved rates of return on diminished resources allocated to schools, many administrators have turned to the private sector for help. Private enterprise has long been espoused and endorsed as the most efficient way to gain maximum output from variable inputs in industry and commerce. Professional educators may be highly competent and expert in administering school instructional programs but may be limited, by virtue of training and experience, in operating ancillary service programs productively. After all, transportation, food service, maintenance, and other ancillary service functions constitute industries and professional career paths of their own.

For these reasons and others, privatization merits consideration to assist you in gaining top results from these complex ancillary components.

A. *Definition of Privatization*

Privatization simply means transferring all or part of the operational responsibility for delivery of services or products from your public school system to a private sector firm, or external provider, under conditions specified through a contractual arrangement. A contract obligates your school system to another party in exchange for a defined benefit. Other terms used to describe privatization include *contracting* and *purchased services*. For example, you might contract with a private firm to provide transportation services to your school district, either with or without ownership of capital equipment or buses. You might also contract with a private firm to clean and maintain your buildings. In complex demographic situations, such as fast-growing suburban communities, professional demographic planning firms have been used to evaluate and identify population trends with school enrollment implications. Many other types of privatization have been gaining in popularity.

B. *Types of Services*

The most frequent form of privatization, or contracting, is in the area of transportation. Food services are another area rapidly growing in popularity for privatization. Other types of services include computer services, custodial services, building and equipment maintenance support, lawn and grounds management, enrollment forecasting, and financial management. Basically, any service needed by the school that is available in the private sector is a candidate for privatization.

C. *When to Consider Privatization*

Several advantages accrue to school districts that employ private sector firms for delivery of services. Examples of these advantages are shown in Table 3.5.

TABLE 3.5 Examples of Advantages in Privatization

Area of Operations	Advantage
Administration	Unfettered administrative time for other tasks, such as teacher supervision
Contractual	Transfer of labor negotiations and contract administration
Employee benefit	Career path opportunities for employees
Equipment	Availability of specialized equipment not easily accessible by schools
Insurance	Transfer of risk (worker's compensation, liability, and so on)
Mission—purpose	Congruence with mission, such as food service company, not school
Personnel	Shift of employment responsibilities (selection, evaluation, and so on)
Personnel	Reduction of benefits administrative responsibilities (leaves, vacation)
Personnel	Improved control in termination of unsatisfactory personnel
Personnel	Responsiveness to fluctuating or seasonal demands for personnel
Purchasing	Economy of scale in purchasing supplies, equipment
Work specialization	Enhancement of performance and efficiency
Work specialization	Greater specialization in skill areas
Work specialization	Improved execution of unique tasks, such as marketing

D. When Not to Consider Privatization

No alternative is best under all conditions, and you might find that privatization is not best for your situation. Privatization probably would not be the best choice in situations when

    operations are functioning efficiently and economically
    no cost advantage would accrue to the school
    operations are instructionally critical
    external providers are not readily available
    labor conditions are healthy or not problematical
    employee job security would be jeopardized by transfer of control
    contract services might disrupt security or operations

E. Asset Ownership

An issue in privatization is that of asset ownership. For example, in privatizing transportation services, the question arises as to which party will own the capital equipment (buses) and facilities (buildings). Your school district might choose to maintain ownership of buses as an insurance hedge against contractor default or termination. In this case, you would contract only for operations while keeping ownership of your bus fleet. Also, you could continue to maintain control over the equipment characteristics such as design, capacity, engine type, and fuel used. Cost benefits and advantages would need to be carefully monitored to determine the efficacy of both options.

Private sector firms operate under different operational motivations and constraints than do public schools. Prudent management on your part should compel you to consider privatization as a possible way you might be able to improve services and also reduce costs.

3.10 Summary

Ancillary services constitute an important set of functions in educational organizations. Although many of the functions are low in profile, they are no less important for smoothly operating schools than more visible parts of the school program. Given appropriate commitment to policy, planning, sound supervision, and use of evaluation for improvement, productivity in ancillary services should contribute to the overall quality of your school.

References

Jordan, K. F., et al. (1987). Risk management and insurance. In *School business administration* (pp. 357-408). Newbury Park, CA: Sage.

Neill, G. (1983). *The local education foundation: A new way to raise money for schools* (NASSP Special Report). Reston, VA: National Association of Secondary School Principals.

Randall, L. H. (1986). Risk management. In R. C. Wood (Ed.), *Principles of school business management* (pp. 345-380). Reston, VA: Association of School Business Officials International.

U.S. Department of Agriculture. (1990). *Meal pattern requirements and offer versus serve manual FNS 265*. Washington, DC: USDA Food and Nutrition Service.

U.S. Department of Agriculture. (1991). *Meal counting and claiming manual FNS 270*. Washington, DC: USDA Food and Nutrition Service.

4

Selecting Instructional Materials That Work and Avoid Censorship Challenges

In this chapter, you will learn how to select instructional materials that work best with your teachers and students and that avoid censorship challenges. This chapter shows you how to have the right written procedures and to assure that those procedures are followed.

AUTHOR'S NOTE: Each section of this chapter and all the figures are fully taught and explained in a manual called, *Textbook Adoption: A Process for Decision-Making*, by Connie Muther. Audio- and videotapes are also available by calling (203) 649-9517 or writing TAAS, Inc., 257 East Center Street, Manchester, CT 06040.

4.1 Decisions to Make Before Beginning

Before you begin to select materials, you need to make several decisions: (a) When will each subject be reviewed? (b) Will money will be available to purchase materials once the selection has been made? (c) Who should be responsible for the selection? (d) How much time will they need to have?

A. *When?*

State a systematic cycle of review of each content area. Seven to eight years is the best cycle of review. Many districts rotate every five or six years, however. This keeps staff too involved in the change process rather than focusing on the effectiveness of the selected materials. But whatever your choice, be sure it is stated clearly.

Sample Cycle of Review

1991: Math
1992: Music/art
1993: Science and technology
1994: Physical education, health
1995: Language arts
1996: Foreign languages
1997: Social studies
1998: Swing year in case an adoption had to be postponed

B. *Cost?*

Provide money so that materials can be purchased once the decision has been made. Many districts run into financial difficulty after the selection committee has been working for months, and the purchase must be put off a year. The message to your faculty is that their time and effort has not been worth it. Morale goes down, and many committee members will refuse to serve again.

Also, publishers work on a two-year revision cycle, with the materials available for review six months or more before the copyright takes effect. This means that, if you examine a book with a 1993 copyright date, it was available almost a year before that date and the publisher is already working on a brand-new or revised program that will be available for examination in 1994 but will carry a 1995 copyright date. Therefore, if you hold off the purchase of the program even for one year, you have essentially wasted all the time, money, and manpower spent evaluating materials.

What should you do? Before beginning to select a subject for this year, include in your policy that the money available for purchase will be put into a reserved budget fund. This protects the money and signals to your staff that their work is valued.

c. *Who?*

Identify a committee that reflects each grade or course and specific student populations. There is no one best size for a committee; however, it should be composed of teachers representing every building and every grade, within reason. Large districts may be unable to do this if the committee becomes too large (60 or more).

The best structure is to require all faculty to serve on one curriculum review/materials selection committee. The committee is responsible for identification of the curriculum, selection of the instructional materials to match that curriculum, and the success of both. It should be a K-12 committee serving for a long period of time: three to five years. This structure allows all educators to view the curriculum from a K-12 perspective. It also means they will understand the importance of both curriculum and measurement. Figure 4.1 is an example of the organization of committee members.

Most districts do not use this structure. Instead, they have a curriculum committee and then create a materials selection committee of different educators (who therefore select materials that do not match the identified curriculum). Success is

LOCATION	GRADE	SPECIALIST	ADMINISTRATION	PARENT BOARD	HOURLY	STUDENT
School A 18 Gidwell St.	6 Reading J. Hanks	Ethel Boyd		(Mrs. Jerry Dow)		
School B 25B Esquire Dr.	K J. Fair		Bob Frankel			
School C 44 Rosylin Rd. 871-3747	4 Librarian T. Jenks 1 N. Howe	Sue Wood				
School D 383 Hubbard Ct.		Talented J. Wright				(Student Council J. Smith)
School E 7 Burlington 871-3748	2 H. Derby 5 T. Rise				(Sec. R. Gagnon)	
School G 20 Sperling 871-3749	7 C. Staub 8 J. Single		*TEXTBOOK ADOPTION ADVISORY SERVICES, INC.* *257 East Center Street, Manchester, Connecticut 06040* (203) 649-9517 (203) 649-9013			
School H 2 Main St. 871-3750	High School D. Laliberti K. Stueifer J. Harper					

©1991 Connie Muther, All rights reserved.

Jim Bennet, Assistant Superintendent for Curriculum and Instruction, will direct the committee.

Please address all questions and concerns to your building representative.
Members included in parentheses are ad hoc members for special assignments.

Figure 4.1. Adoption Committee Members

based on standardized tests and publishers' testing rather than on the expected curriculum outcomes.

If you are going to have a curriculum that is taught and learned, then all educators must know what it is and be able to select those topics, concepts, or skills from the materials provided that match that curriculum. You also need to provide some sort of valid measurement of that curriculum.

D. *What?*

Provide a plan or process with completion dates and monitor to be sure that the plan has been followed. On the typical textbook selection committee, everyone evaluates everything for their own purposes. Meetings run overtime. Arguments are rampant. Finally, the decision must be made because the deadline for purchase has come. The decision can then be based on of the attractiveness of the covers, the spiral- (or hard-) bound teachers' editions, a favorite author, the personality of the sales agent, and the free materials that are given away. This is not a decision based on whether the materials will work for your students and help implement your curriculum.

Therefore you must have a *plan,* with fixed completion dates, of *what* will happen, *when* it will happen, and *who* will do it. The committee, with training if they are new to this process, will decide *how* it will happen.

4.2 Developing the Materials Selection Process Plan

There are three parts to a materials selection plan (see Figure 4.2). The first is planning, analyzing, and identifying what you most want and need. If you don't know what you want, how can you know what to look for—and how will you know if you've found it? The second part is objectively evaluating and scientifically selecting the materials that most closely match what you want and need. The third and most critical stage is implementing and correcting, or getting those who were not involved in the

Selecting Instructional Materials 69

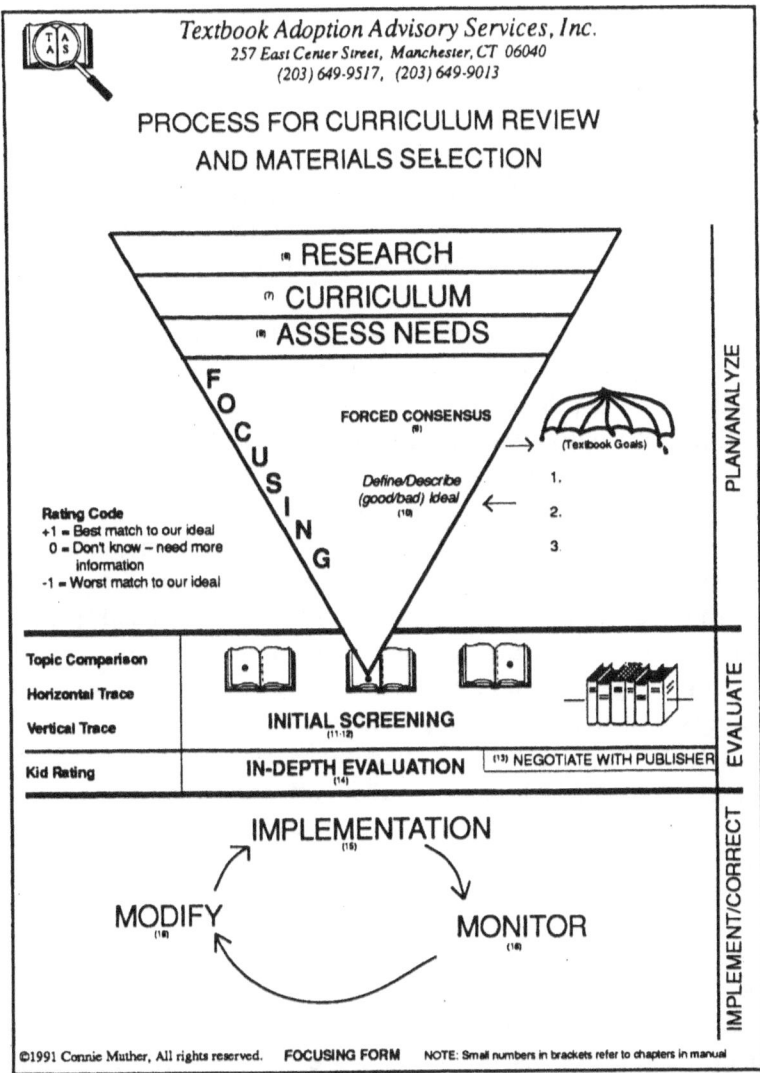

Figure 4.2. An Outline of the Process

selection decision to accept and use the new materials effectively. It is this final stage that is often neglected by many districts.

Each segment of the process, with a recommended amount of time, is explained below.

A. *Research*

Time: Three to six months. Research means finding what works. What are the latest issues and trends that are known to improve student learning in the subject of study? Publishers publish what sells. What sells and what works are not synonymous.

We, as consumers, purchase what is comfortable, what is familiar. We resist change. Mentally open your closet. What kind of clothes do you buy? How often do you change your brand of toothpaste? Publishers know research results but are prevented from really incorporating them into new materials for fear it will not look familiar to the buyer.

Therefore have the committee spend time reviewing the new methods that work, so they'll be able to identify them when they see them in published materials. You can easily obtain this research by giving one teacher on your committee the gift of membership in the national subject area association along with the requirement that he or she provide a review of it. Also, contact your local state education department consultant and university professors. Ask them to identify just one or two articles that best summarize what works in the selected subject. Collect only the best; then summarize the results.

B. *Curriculum Design*

Time: One to two years. Publishers publish what sells. This means they must include everything everyone wants. Most districts use standardized tests, so publishers must include all topics and skills tested on all these tests to prevent their materials from being eliminated. More than 40 states now require state testing so all those skills must also be included. Everyone has favorite topics, so these too, must be included. The results are

Selecting Instructional Materials 71

textbooks with more than 600 pages that kids can't even carry home from school.

Long before you begin to evaluate instructional materials, you must have a statement of curriculum, or *exit outcomes*. What will your students be able to do at the end each course and grade that they were not able to do when they entered it? If you do not identify expected outcomes, what will you evaluate the new instructional materials against?

C. Assessment of Needs

Time: One to two weeks. There are two needs to assess before looking at any new materials: (a) *the student's weakest area in a subject* and (b) *the way the current instructional materials are being used.*

Your goal in selection of materials is to improve both instruction and learning. By focusing your evaluation on selecting materials that are the best in your students' weakest area, you'll accomplish both. Because the truth is that the students' weakest area is also the teachers' weakest area.

A change in textbook will *not* change the way the textbook is used, therefore you need to identify the typical use of the textbook. Then, during evaluation, if you select materials that should be used differently, you'll be so aware of it you will also provide a system for training in how to use the new materials.

For example, many hands-on materials failed some years ago, not because the materials were at fault but because the teachers were not shown how to use them as they were designed to be used.

D. Ranking to Determine What to Evaluate

Time: One to two weeks. There are hundreds of things on which you can evaluate instructional materials. The task is to reduce the possibilities to the two or three most important criteria. For example, which is most important to evaluate in *social studies* materials:

(a) the quality of the writing so your students can read, understand, and remember the information present;
(b) that the information is accurate;
(c) that the information is so well organized that you can find and extract what matches your curriculum exit outcomes;
(d) that the material presents critical thinking and problem solving; or
(e) that geography is integrated so that the map, chart, and graph instruction also complements the history presented?

There are many other things worth considering.

It is important to list all options and have all faculty rank them. One quick and simple ranking system is shown in Figure 4.3. Real decision making is produced with this technique, and it yields a numerical result. If everyone has the same number of points and is given the opportunity to participate, they cannot successfully challenge the results.

The key to success throughout the evaluation of materials is this agreed-upon forced ranking. Then the subsequent screening evaluation of materials focuses only on what has been identified.

If you have a difficult and quarrelsome group in your district who may oppose the final selection decision, be sure to include them in this forced ranking. When you do, you can later show that they had equal opportunity to participate.

E. *Define and Describe Criteria Identified by Forced Ranking and Practice Evaluating on Good/Bad Lessons*

Time: One day of released time per criterion. Suppose critical thinking and problem solving were identified as top-rated criteria. Everyone in your district may have a different idea of what that means. You need to spend several hours defining and describing each criterion, then practice evaluating them on existing materials to ensure everyone will clearly recognize what the quality is when they see it.

At least one day of released time must be scheduled for this because it is a difficult undertaking. Enormous thought is

Fill In This Form

TECHNIQUE FOR PRIORITIZING CRITERIA

1. List criteria.
2. Multiply number of criteria by 1 1/2. Result is total number any evaluator may use.
3. Rate criteria on 0-3 scale with 0=low, 3=high.
  (The total score may not exceed the total from number 2 above)
  By placing a ceiling on the total number of points allowed, the results will be more consistent.

List Criteria	Assign Rating 0-3
1.	____
2.	____
3.	____
4.	____
5.	____
6.	____
7.	____
8.	____

©1991 Connie Muther. All rights reserved.

Example of a Completed Form

TECHNIQUE FOR PRIORITIZING CRITERIA

1. List criteria.
2. Multiply number of criteria by 1 1/2. Result is total number any evaluator may use. (12)
3. Rate criteria on 0-3 scale with 0=low, 3=high.
  By placing a ceiling on the total number of points allowed, the results will be more consistent.

List Criteria	Assign Rating 0-3	TOTAL Add Results From All Evaluations
1. Strong Comprehension	3	(9)#1
2. Vocabulary Development	0	(7)#3
3. Motivating Pictures	0	3
4. Reading in Content Areas	3	60
5. Critical Thinking	3	(8)#2
6. Application to longer piece of discourse	2	59
7. Writing and Reading	1	30
8. Strong Decoding	0	8
9.		Total: 408
10.		
11.	Total: 12	34 Responses from gr. 7 & 8

TEXTBOOK ADOPTION ADVISORY SERVICES, INC.
257 East Center Street, Manchester, Connecticut 06040
(203) 649-9517   (203) 649-9013

Figure 4.3. Sample Technique for Ranking Criteria

required, and members of the committee must have the opportunity to listen to and understand what their peers are saying.

Use a "good/bad" form that lists both good and bad characteristics of your identified criterion. Ask each committee member to find examples of the best example and the worst example from any existing materials. List and photocopy them for distribution to all committee members for evaluation. As each example is discussed, the committee must agree that it is good, or bad, and why. The rationale must refer back to the characteristics listed on the good/bad form.

Figure 4.4 is an example of "clear writing" in social studies.

F. Evaluate Materials for Initial Screening

Time: One week of summer work or several days and/or afternoons during the year. Initial screening means examining all submitted materials and selecting the three best, which will then be examined more fully. Three generic initial screening strategies that best dissect instructional materials are topic comparison, vertical trace, and horizontal trace. Each of these requires training and practice. If this is the committee's first introduction to the strategies, time must be provided. Once they know how to do the strategies, they can be done more quickly.

Topic comparison compares exactly the same topic, concept, or skill in all textbook submissions at the same grade level. The topic comparison is the easiest evaluation strategy to do and lays the foundation for all others. It is the weakest evaluation, however, in that it looks at too small a sample of the textbook. So, begin your evaluation with this strategy. Once your committee understands how to do a topic comparison, move quickly into the vertical trace.

The *vertical trace* evaluates the vertical development of one topic, concept, or skill throughout several grades of the same publisher's series, that is, a topic comparison vertically through the grades. The vertical trace is your most powerful evaluation to get educators to realize that the textbook should never be the curriculum. One vertical trace per publisher is recommended.

Selecting Instructional Materials 75

DEFINE/DESCRIBE YOUR IDEAL:	**CLEAR WRITING**

GOOD	**BAD**
STUDENTS WILL BE ABLE TO READ, UNDERSTAND, AND REMEMBER THE TEXT	
• It must be interesting to kids!	• Too many topics, too many facts superficially covered ("mentioning")
• Words create visual images in the mind of the reader	
• Structure of writing is easily recognized (i.e., compare/contrast, list, cause/effect)	• Too many or unrelated graphics = distraction from the flow of the text
• Sequencing is logical	• Vocabulary too difficult, unfamiliar, no context clues
• Avoids irrelevant information	• "Dumbing down" to fit readability formulas
• Good contextual clues (i.e., meaning defined in context, examples provided . . .)	• Too many concepts
• Transitional words truly give transition: but, so, if . . .	• Boring
• What is introduced is reinforced	
• Appropriate background information is provided	**TEXTBOOK ADOPTION ADVISORY SERVICES, INC.** *257 East Center Street Manchester, Connecticut 06040 (203) 649-9517 (203) 649-9013*
• Little or no rereading required	©1991 Connie Muther, All rights reserved.

Figure 4.4. Good/Bad Form for Clear Writing

The *horizontal trace* compares the total development of one topic, concept, or skill in one course including the testing. This is the most comprehensive strategy because it looks at large chunks of the publisher's material. It is the best evaluation for all types of instructional materials, including hands-on, interactive video, and computer programs. The horizontal trace takes the longest to do, however. Two per publisher is the minimum recommended.

The topic, concept, or skill examined should be only those that (a) are essential to your curriculum (which you identified previously), (b) were identified as the students' weakest area (you identified this when you did your needs assessment), and (c) reflect what was defined on the good/bad form. For example, in social studies, in Figure 4.4, the forced ranking determined clear writing would be evaluated. Any topic that is essential to your curriculum that is also the students' weakest area can be selected.

How to do the topic comparison. Select a topic. In the example in Figure 4.5, the Boston Massacre was chosen for fifth grade as it is small enough to reproduce as a topic comparison. Then open all textbook submissions to the Boston Massacre to determine which one is most clearly written.

This sounds simple, but trying to determine which is best when you're looking at so many is highly difficult. Therefore designate each publisher with a color code. Then photocopy each publisher's version on the assigned color of paper. Select three versions to cut and tape and lay out side by side to easily determine the differences.

Once your display is made, photocopy the original layout so everyone on the committee can read it too. This presents unbiased evidence on what each publisher offers. Because everyone is looking at the same content, they have a vehicle to discuss and determine which publisher's version best matched what they defined as good, as in Figure 4.4. When someone evaluates for irrelevant information—"but I don't like the typeface"—it cannot be accepted as evidence because it does not refer to what was on the good/bad form.

These photocopied examples can then be shared with faculty who are not on the committee. But when you share them, you must also share the good/bad definition so that they too are

THREE PUBLISHERS SIDE-BY-SIDE

TOPIC: BOSTON MASSACRE	COURSE: SOCIAL STUDIES	GRADE: 5
GOLD-E p.99	BEIGE-E p.190	YELLOW-E p.100
THE BOSTON MASSACRE	THE BOSTON MASSACRE	THE BOSTON MASSACRE
On March 5, 1770, some colonists surrounded a British soldier and started throwing snowballs at him. They shouted "Redcoat!" and "Lobsterback!" at him. More soldiers ran to help and before long they started to shoot into the crowd. Five colonists were killed and a lot more were wounded. This was called the Boston Massacre and it led the Sons of Liberty to set up committees of correspondence in all of the colonies so that everyone could know what had happened.	British soldiers had been in Boston for two years. Part of the reason they were there was to make sure that the colonists paid taxes to Britain. This made the people very angry because they did not want Britain interfering with the way they ran the colonies. One snowy March night in 1770, a crowd gathered around a lone British soldier. This soldier was guarding the building where the British collected taxes from the colonists. The colonists began to insult the soldier, shouting, "Redcoat!" and "Lobsterback!" Then they threw snowballs and pieces of ice at him. The soldier became frightened and shouted for help. A British officer and some more soldiers heard and came running. The officer ordered the soldiers not to shoot, but the crowd got bigger and the colonists now carried axes, clubs, and guns. The soldiers fired into the crowd to protect themselves. Three colonists were instantly killed. Two others died later. One of the dead was a freed slave, named Crispus Attucks. This ugly event quickly became known as the Boston Massacre. It made more and more colonists even angrier at the British.	At night on March 5th, 1770, British soldiers were guarding a building on a Boston street when a group of colonists gathered around them. The colonists started to throw insults and snowballs at them. They called for help; more soldiers arrived. The colonists kept throwing things at the soldiers, until the soldiers fired their guns into the crowd. Five colonists died and more were wounded. This event was called the Boston Massacre.

TEXTBOOK ADOPTION ADVISORY SERVICES, INC.
257 East Center Street, Manchester, Connecticut 06040
(203) 649-9517   (203) 649-9013

©1991 Connie Muther, All rights reserved.

Figure 4.5. Example of Cut and Tape

focused on what quality is. This prevents pulling in something irrelevant. You can also use these cut and tapes with students, especially if you're evaluating for clear writing. Just as with teachers, students should be directed to show *why* they feel one version is best. It's their reasoning that tells you specifically on what they are focusing.

How to do a vertical trace. The topic comparison prepares the way for learning how to do a vertical trace. Select a topic, concept, or skill that should be developed sequentially throughout several grades based on the identified curriculum. You may again want to focus on something that is your students' weakest area. Locate in the indexes or tables of contents where it is taught in each publisher's series.

Put each publisher's book on a separate table opened to the first lesson of that specific topic for each sequential grade you have chosen. Examine the lessons displayed and try to identify the trend within one publisher. Photocopy what represents the trend, then lay these photocopies side by side so you can easily determine the progression to see if they expand and become more and more challenging or if they repeat the same information. The example provided (see Figure 4.6) is from a best-selling high school English composition publisher.

Again, because it is easier to work with only three publishers, cluster publishers into triads. Using the same color-coding system for each publisher, photocopy the lessons that demonstrate the trend you've observed. Determine which of the three publishers' materials best matches what you've defined and described you wanted on the good/bad form.

How to do a horizontal trace. In the vertical trace, several grades were examined, but the horizontal trace will require only one grade. As in the other evaluation strategies, select a topic, concept, or skill that is essential to your curriculum or is one of your students' weakest areas. The area selected should reflect one of the criteria identified by the forced ranking. In the horizontal trace, start with an exit outcome (how you measure success

Selecting Instructional Materials 79

Writing a Description, Grades 9 - 12.
Side-by-side One Publisher Display

Grade	Grade 9	Grade 10	Grade 11	Grade 12
Title	Writing A Description: Descriptive Language	Writing A Description: Descriptive Language	Writing A Description: Descriptive Language	Writing A Description: Descriptive Language
Definition	Effective descriptive writing uses exact and vivid language.	Effective descriptive writing uses exact and vivid language.	Effective descriptive writing uses exact and vivid language.	Effective descriptive writing uses exact and vivid language.
Explanation	If you want your readers to know how the subject you describe looks, sounds, smells, tastes, or feels, you will have to choose your words carefully and place them exactly. By exercising such care in choosing and placing words, you will make your description vivid. In addition, the precise words you choose will place your individual stamp on your writing.	In order to pinpoint just how your subject looks, sounds, smells, and feels, you need to pick and place your words exactly. As a result, your writing will become vivid almost automatically, for precise language gives descriptive writing an individual spark and twist.	NONE!	In order to describe your subject as you experienced or imagined it, you need to select and place your words exactly. Your writing will thereby become vivid almost without conscious effort, because precise language gives descriptive writing an individual flavor and twist.
Instruction	When it comes time to choose between two similar words to use in a description, keep the following suggestions in mind. If you want to know more about any of these suggestions, refer to Chapter 5. 1. Always choose the most specific word. General: The *building* stood on the *place* like a silent sentinel. Specific: The *castle* stood on the *cliff* like a silent sentinel.	Keep in mind the following points when you are choosing between two similar words for descriptive writing. For more information about any of the points, see Chapter 5. 1. Always, always, always pick the most specific word. General: I would start out in the *boat* in the long shadows of the *trees*. Specific: I would ... start out in the *canoe* ... in the long shadows of the *pines*. – E.B. White	Remember the following points when you are choosing words for descriptive writing. For more information about any of these points, see Chapter 5. 1. Always pick the most specific word. General: The *bird* soared over the grove of barren *trees*. More Specific: The *eagle* soared over the grove of barren *maples*.	When you are choosing between two similar words for descriptive writing, keep in mind the following points. For more information about any of these points, see Chapter 5. 1. Always select the most specific word. General: The *people* were splendid *artists*. Specific: The *Egyptians* were splendid *potraitists*. – Ariane Ruskin
Activity	Exercise 9. Using Descriptive Language. Rewrite the following paragraph using more exact and vivid language. Use figures of speech in at least one sentence. Feel free to combine any sentences as you see fit. Paul stopped rowing to look at the sunset. It was as pretty as a picture. A group of birds moved just over the water one last time before going to their roosting places. Shadows of the trees were on the water of the lake. Behind the trees the sun looked beautiful. A shiny fish came out of the water near Paul's boat. It scared him. Everything was so quiet. When it got dark Paul took the boat back to shore. He had a good feeling.	Exercise 10. Using Descriptive Language. Rewrite the following paragraph using more exact and vivid language. Use figures of speech in at least one sentence. Feel free to combine any sentences as you see fit. Our group climbed to the mountain top. Fred and I moved ahead of the others, yelling our heads off when we caught sight of the mountain top. The view that we saw at the top of the mountain was very colorful. The clouds below us looked nice. The sky around us was blue. We all enjoyed the experience a great deal.	Exercise 11. Using Descriptive Language. Rewrite the following paragraph using more exact words and vivid language. Use a figure of speech in at least one sentence. Combine any sentences as you see fit. Our rubber raft went quickly down the fast river. Cliffs of the surrounding gorge sped by like blinking lights. The current carried us rapidly. The raft moved up and down over the foamy waves and rocks. Then we entered a quiet piece of still water. The peace was nice. Finally we were as safe as a doorknob.	Exercise 11. Using Descriptive Language. Rewrite the following paragraph using more exact and vivid language. Use a figure of speech in at least one sentence. Feel free to combine sentences as you see fit. Camping out was a good experience. First we set up our tent and put some things into it. We then got some wood and made a fire. Next we cooked dinner, which turned out to be very good. After our meal we sat around the fire, sang some nice songs, and shot the breeze for awhile before turning in.

TEXTBOOK ADOPTION ADVISORY SERVICES, INC.
257 East Center Street, Manchester, Connecticut 06040
(203) 649-9517   (203) 649-9013

Figure 4.6. Vertical Trace Example: English Textbook

for students in this topic at one grade level). Ideally, district testing measures the curriculum's exit outcomes, so starting there is best. If there is no district curriculum testing, begin with the publisher's tests or end of chapter questions for the one topic you've selected.

First, take the test yourself. List what you need to know to pass the test. Then, using the publishers' index, trace through all the instruction and presentation of that one topic until you reach the point where you would administer the test. Determine whether the instruction presented will teach the students what they need to know in order to be successful with the test.

As with all the initial screening strategies, evaluate three publishers together and determine which is the best of the three before looking at three more.

Figure 4.7 summarizes the three text evaluation strategies with definitions, procedures, and minimum recommendations.

G. *Why the Evaluation Strategies Work*

To understand why these strategies work, it's important to know how publishers create a textbook program. Because there is a two-year revision cycle, there is very little time to put a series together. Therefore 100-150 writers must work all at the same time, often in different cities, and sometimes not even talking with one another, trying to crank out all the components of a major series. One writer may be writing the chapter, while a different person writes the questions to that chapter. But the questioner does not have the written chapter to work from and must therefore write the questions on the subtitles. Another writer may be writing the objectives, again in isolation from the person who writes the content and the questions. Someone else writes the information in the teacher's edition; another writes the workbook sheets. It's easy to see the possibilities for error.

How content is selected. Long before the writers begin, the marketing staff in each publishing house decides what the new textbook series will look like. They spend long hours determining

Selecting Instructional Materials   81

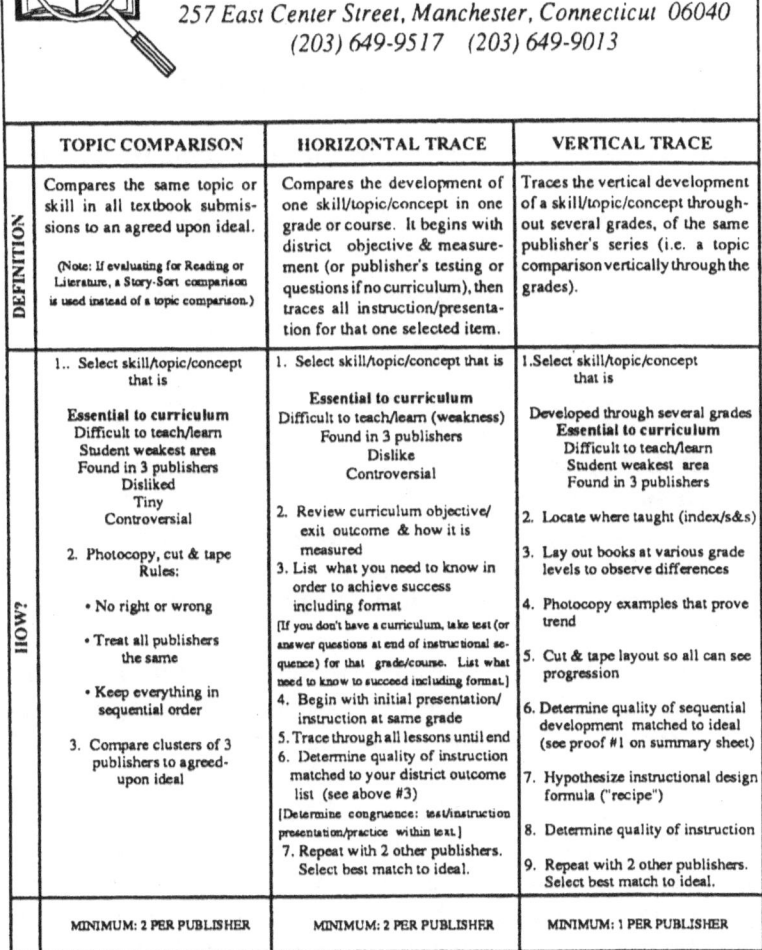

Figure 4.7. Combining Text Evaluations

what to provide so the program will be a best-seller. It's similar to an apple pie contest: What ingredients should we include in our winning recipe? But, with publishers, the recipe is called "the instructional design formula." Sometimes senior authors are called in to help determine this recipe, but too often they are not.

Very simply, an instructional design for social studies might be similar to a shopping list:

1. Each chapter will have six lessons followed by review and testing.
2. Each lesson will be three pages long, opening with a list of objectives.
3. Vocabulary words will be italicized and boldfaced with definitions provided on sidebars.
4. Six questions will follow each lesson: four fill-in-the-blank, one interpretive, and a final one called "critical thinking" for discussion.
5. Answers may not vary, so specific suggestions must be provided for all questions.
6. Each chapter will open with a time line and a four-color art photo on the right-hand side.
7. A map will appear every three pages along with boxed and highlighted additional information related to minority issues or whatever issues are popular at the time of publication.

The project is then farmed out to writers, many of whom work in "development houses" and write social studies programs for several competing publishers at the same time. It is easy to see how these evaluation strategies work and that you do not have to do very many of them. With a vertical trace, you can quickly see whether the same information is being presented repeatedly for one topic, concept, or skill. If it is, then it's probably being repeated for the others as this must be that publisher's instructional design recipe. In a horizontal trace, you will immediately learn whether the questions can be answered by the instruction presented. If you do two horizontal traces, one at second grade and another at seventh grade, and you find the same format, you can randomly open up any other grade to check to see whether you've identified the instructional design recipe.

Selecting Instructional Materials 83

4.3 Organizing Publisher Data to Get Down to the Best Three

As publishers submit sample materials, color code and tag only the *core* items, which are the components evaluated in the initial screening. The core is whatever most influences day-to-day instruction in your districts' classrooms. In most cases, the core is just the pupil text.

Then, set up a planning form that identifies publishers' colors, the evaluation types, and the topics evaluated. Figure 4.8 is an example of such a planning form. An important task is to review the evaluation form to ensure that each publisher has been evaluated equally.

A. *Using a Rating System to Narrow Choices to the Three Best*

The recommended rating system is designed to quickly identify and focus on the best programs rather than to emphasize the worst. Therefore, if one program is obviously better than the others, it is given a +1, and the others automatically get a −1. The zero is used only when there's disagreement between evaluators or when one textbook does not provide enough information (e.g., your topic of evaluation is the Boston Massacre, and the textbook being evaluated does not have anything on it). A zero acts as a plus in that it means you must look at the program again, which increases the number of evaluation reports and therefore your time.

Rating System:

+1 = Good: Best matches your ideal
 0 = Not enough information in the lesson selected or can't reach consensus between evaluators
−1 = Another program is better: This does not match your ideal

Figure 4.8. Initial Screening

If the committee is in real disagreement and the discussion is not leading to improved instruction, give a zero. This saves time and headaches. But it does mean the program must be evaluated again for a different topic, concept, skill, or lesson. If all three programs being evaluated are awful, one still must get a plus. If none of the programs merits a plus, assign +1C ("conditional"). This signals "forced plus" to all committee members and full value is never given. Only one conditional plus rating can be given in an evaluation report. The others receive a minus.

Likewise, if all programs are wonderful and you feel they should all receive a +1, you must give a -1C to one of the programs. Again, when you see the conditional rating, you know it was forced.

Rules are simple. Each triad must have at least one plus. It may have two pluses, but not three. Likewise, each report must have at least one minus, though it may have two, but not three. The purpose for initial screening evaluation is to eliminate the worst programs and retain the best for further study, called "in-depth evaluation." The fewer pluses given, the quicker your initial screening evaluation will be completed. The programs with the most pluses are compared with each other until you have only three left.

4.4 Working With Publishers' Representatives and Handling Sample Materials

The sales agent may be your best friend and should be treated as the professional he or she is. Yet, you must also realize that the purpose of selling is to entice you to buy. So it may not be possible to remain friendly with agents and be unbiased.

When you request sample copies of materials, the agent should be informed that the study will be a "closed adoption." This means that the agent may not be in contact with anyone on your committee and must deal only with you. If any agent should contact anyone on the committee, their product may be eliminated from consideration. By conducting a closed adoption, you prevent the committee from being swayed by fancy sales pitches or bribes. Agents also need to know that the administrator's role is as an unbiased, nonvoting facilitator of the adoption. This gives freedom to remain friends with publishers' representatives while ensuring a fair selection decision by the committee.

When requesting sample copies of materials, there are two items you need to obtain from each publisher: (a) copies of each publisher's replacement and rebinding policy and (b) samples of service proposals.

Replacement and rebinding policy. Eighty percent of the major publishers in the United States use the same five printers. This means that competing publishers' books are being bound by the same machines. Each publisher has a contract with its printer that, if the books you purchase fall apart within a specified amount of time, the printer will replace or rebind them at no charge. You should obtain copies of all policies from every publisher, select the best policy, and negotiate with the winning publisher to provide you with the terms of the best policy.

Service proposals. Publishers offer consultant services free of charge to large purchasers. What they offer is presented as a "service proposal." Small purchasers may request these too. If publishers will not provide you support and service when you are selecting materials, they probably will not be there to help when you have problems. Collect all service proposals, analyze them, and write your own, reflecting what your district needs.

Publisher negotiations. It's best to negotiate with the publisher when the competition is most high. In this process, competition is highest after initial screening down to the three best programs. For assurance of delivery on promises, signatures should be required on all contracts with publishers, including those of the sales representative, the regional manager, and a senior vice president.

Selecting Instructional Materials 87

A. *Publisher's Contracts That Should Be Obtained*

1. A contract that states all the bits and pieces of any program you are purchasing must be available for the life of your adoption. State the life of your adoption: Anywhere from five to ten years is realistic. If you have this contract, the publisher cannot drop its books into out-of-print status within the specified time period.

2. The best replacement and rebinding policy (see above) must be negotiated.

3. A service contract also must be negotiated, with specified dates of services provided to your district (see above).

4. A sealed proposal of all free items from each publisher must be provided. Publishers may not reduce the price of a textbook; however, they can reduce the bottom line by providing free textbooks. A sealed proposal is not a sealed bid. A sealed bid implies you will select the lowest bidder. A sealed proposal means that you will neither negotiate with the publisher nor automatically accept with the lowest price. Rather, you will select the instructional materials that best match what your district most wants and needs. Once the proposals are opened, the second- or third-ranked program may have the "best deal," so ask the committee to determine whether the second or third choice is a better option because of a lower price.

By asking for sealed proposals, and letting the committee decide, both publishers and committee members are treated as professionals. Moreover, this selection procedure ultimately rewards those publishers who produce the best quality product. Unfortunately, many educators today go to the publishers in search of the "best deal," negotiate for price, and ultimately undermine the work of the committee. Such practice sends a signal to publishers that educators do not care about the quality of the product; they are only concerned about "the freebies."

4.5 Conducting the In-Depth Evaluation

Time: Two to six months. Once most publishers have been eliminated, and the best three are left, the evaluation is opened up to examine more than just the topic comparison and horizontal and vertical traces. The two best methods for the in-depth evaluation are visitations to user-schools and "Kid-Ratings."

A user-school is one that has been using the publishers' product for more than a year. You simply obtain names and telephone numbers of these users from the publisher. Call to see whether they are using the exact components you wish to purchase and have a similar student population. Visit the user-schools that are most similar to yours to see how well the program is going.

In Kid-Ratings, the students determine which of the three publishers' texts best teaches them what they need to know to pass a teacher-provided pretest. To do a Kid-Rating, select a topic, concept, or skill that has not yet been taught for one grade or course. It should be the next topic the teacher plans to teach from your district curriculum. In this way, you are not experimenting with students unless it directly relates to your curriculum.

Prepare a pretest of what students need to learn. Photocopy the lesson from each of the three publishers and mark them A, B, and C. Give the students the pretest, explaining to them that they will be helping you select the best materials to teach them what they need to know to pass the pretest.

Divide the class into groups with three students in each. Give one photocopied lesson from one of the three publishers to each person in the group. When the students finish reading their version, they rotate to read the other two versions until all three students have read all three lessons. Then, in their groups, the students must come to agreement as to which publisher's version best taught them what they needed to know to pass the pretest—and why. The reasons they cite are critical.

Many districts nationwide have reported that students often select a different book than the one the committee selected. Often the reasons students give are so sound that the books selected by students are purchased. In several districts, student-selected materials have been more successful than teacher-selected materials.

Why is this so? Teachers often know so much about a subject that they may be unable to see gaps in a presentation, for they automatically provide the missing or obscure information. For example, one group of 65 teachers determined one mathematics lesson was the best choice, but students later said otherwise. The lesson was on equivalent fractions for third grade, and students pointed to a graphic they could not understand. The graphic was of a car gas gauge showing a gas tank and then full of gas. What we learned from students was that third graders could not understand what a picture of a gas gauge meant. Not one adult saw this until students pointed it out. The student perspective is critical.

4.6 Selecting the Best Publisher

Compile all the information for each publisher from all the Kid-Ratings and visits to user-schools. It is usually very clear which program is best, and the selection is unanimous. If this does not happen, simply select the one with the problem that is easiest to fix. Suppose two programs are the best, yet one has poor descriptions of concepts for students and the other has poor testing. Which of the two is easier to fix? Rewriting the testing is easier than rewriting the descriptions in the textbook.

If the committee is still deadlocked, have a vote. Majority wins. It is usually clear which is best, however, and everyone normally agrees.

4.7 Presenting the Recommendation to the School Board for Approval

Once the selection decision is made, the committee must present the selection to the school board for approval. This should be scheduled near the end of March so the purchase order can be received by the publisher before April 15. Sometimes districts send their purchase orders in so late that their order is placed on "back order" and the books will arrive too late for September use.

School boards tend to want a guarantee of two things: low cost and workability with students. In presenting your selection, simply go through the process chart with them (see Figure 4.2) and provide examples of everything done in the process. Because the initial screening is photocopied anyway, select a few clear examples of topic comparisons and vertical and horizontal traces showing the differences between the selected program and those that were eliminated. A brief report of results from user-schools and a presentation from one or two students reporting the results from Kid-Ratings will be all that is needed.

Keeping costs down can be demonstrated with the contracts obtained from publishers.

School boards often do not need much, but documentation throughout the entire process with photocopied proof is needed. If contested, it can clearly demonstrate that the selection was based on solid evidence.

4.8 Handling Challenges to Selected Materials

Challenges to instructional materials have increased dramatically over the years and to such an extent that plans should assume that selections will be challenged. Challenges, however, can only win in districts where bias or coercion is shown. If you have a stated process based on research and selection of materials to match curriculum goals (see Figure 4.2), and can provide evidence of implementation of this process, problems should be minimal. Use of consensus techniques and photocopied examples of evaluations will also help avoid any problems. The process just delineated provides the solution if you document that you followed it.

4.9 Implementing the Use of the New Materials

Time: Ongoing for the life of your adoption. Getting those who were not on your selection committee to accept the final selection decision may be difficult without involvement. Embedded within this process are procedures to involve others. Every teacher in your district should have a copy of the district curriculum, and the evaluation of materials focuses only on those topics, concepts, and skills that are essential to that curriculum. By keeping all your cut-and-taped photocopied evaluations, you can quickly demonstrate why a particular decision was made.

Every teacher in your district should have been involved in the forced consensus steps. This was their opportunity to have a voice in what was evaluated. Teachers not on the committee should also help with the Kid-Ratings collection.

Finally, if there is resistance to the materials selected—and there always will be some no matter what method was used—ask the resistors to help you by critiquing each lesson of the newly selected materials. Assure them they may be right, for *there are no perfect instructional materials*. The only way to have a successful adoption is to listen to all users, to provide them with a response to their concerns, and to modify selected materials for use by the unique students and faculty in your district.

4.10 Assuring Selected Materials Will Work

There is only one way selected materials will work: Monitor and adapt them so they do match local curriculum needs. Because the selection committee is composed of teachers from every building who serve for a minimum of three years, they should be available to monitor (listen) to comments in their building and concerns of teachers, students, and parents. A simple monitoring system involves asking, on an individual basis, "How's the program going?" This is direct and open ended. The monitor simply documents verbatim responses. These responses, comments, and concerns will identify problems before they erupt.

The committee should continue to meet once a month for the life of the adoption, relating any comments and determining how to respond (see Figure 4.9). A system of listening, responding, and *adjusting* will ensure that the materials will meet district needs.

Remember, there is no material or program that can be installed without adaptation. Any choice will ultimately have to be modified based upon information the committee gathers throughout the life of the adoption.

TEXTBOOK ADOPTION SCHEDULE

NOTE: Event numbers are the same as manual chapter numbers

TEXTBOOK ADOPTION ADVISORY SERVICES, INC.
257 East Center Street, Manchester, Connecticut 06040
(203) 649-9517 (203) 649-9013

COMPLETED EVENTS	AUG	SEPT	OCT	NOV	DEC	JAN	FEB	MAR	APR	MAY	JUN	JULY	AUG	SEPT	OCT	NOV	DEC	JAN	FEB	MAR
3. DECISIONS BEFORE BEGINNING		•																		
4. FORM COMMITTEE				•																
6. REVIEW RESEARCH				•——	——•															
7. IDENTIFY ESSENTIAL CURRICULUM						Curriculum revision only														
8. ASSESS NEEDS								•												
9. FORCED CONSENSUS										•										
10. DEFINE/DESCRIBE IDEAL (TRAINING HOW)								Training/evaluating completed at same time ••			••									
11. EVALUATION: INITIAL SCREENING																				
13. NEGOTIATE WITH PUBLISHERS								Director handles all negotiations				•								
14. EVALUATION: IN-DEPTH																		•		
>> ORDER NEW MATERIALS																				
15. IMPLEMENTATION								•												
16. MONITOR														•	•	•	•	•	•	•
16. MODIFY								Modifying is scheduled for summer after use of program and continues for life of adoption, as needed.												

©1991 Connie Mather All rights reserved.

4.11 Library Standards and Management

A qualified librarian is an important person in the instructional program of any school. A librarian should be looked upon as a resource to both staff and students, not as a "keeper of materials." A well-stocked, adequately staffed library/instructional media center/learning center can truly be the "center" of the school's instructional program.

How does a principal determine whether the library is fulfilling its designated function? A principal would do well to look at a recent publication, as well as videotape, prepared by the American Association of School Librarians (AASL) and the Association for Educational Communications and Technology (AECT), *Information Power: Guidelines for School Library Media Programs*. These guidelines, according to the introduction, "point the way to developing programs to prepare students for personal success in the next century."

The book begins with a mission statement to ensure that students and staff are effective users of ideas and information. The individual chapters, complete with helpful bibliographies, discuss programs; roles and responsibilities; leadership, planning, and management; personnel; resources and equipment; facilities; and district, regional, and state leadership. Appendixes include quantitative data on programs from the U.S. Department of Education, sample budget formulas for materials and equipment, space recommendations, a bibliography of selected research, and a series of AASL and AECT policy statements. *Information Power*, Appendix D, "Policies and Statements on Access to Information," includes material that should be incorporated into a district instructional/library materials selection policy.

All policy statements must be written with the following principles that help to determine selection objectives: Resources must

- be appropriate to the education program,
- represent diverse points of view, and
- stimulate growth in analytical and thinking skills.

These objectives apply to all forms of information: books, pamphlets, periodicals, microfilms, data bases, computer software, laser discs, videos, films, and all other media forms. All schools within a district must adhere to a common, districtwide selection policy that has been adopted by the board of education as official district policy. The district instructional materials selection policy also establishes procedures for handling challenges to library and educational materials. It is expected that all members of the community and staff (including administrative staff and board members) adhere to the procedures established for handling challenges or objections to library and educational materials.

If you find yourself in a school without a qualified librarian, it is still important for students and staff to have access to quality materials that will support the curriculum. It is imperative that the person(s) responsible for selecting instructional and library materials does not rely solely upon vendors or publishers' catalogs or their sales representatives. There are unbiased selection aids to help locate quality library materials. An example of those aids are the publications put out by H. W. Wilson Company. They include "Children's Catalog," "Junior High School Library Catalog," and the "Senior High School Library Catalog." No book, even those as helpful as *Information Power* and the standard catalogs published by the H. W. Wilson Company, however, can take the place of a qualified librarian who can be a dynamic force in your school's instructional program.

4.12 Summary

Establish a K-12 committee that serves for at least three years, if not more, to identify the curriculum, select the materials to match that curriculum, and become responsible for the success of both. Involve all teachers in your district in the forced consensus technique. Ensure that all evaluations demonstrate that consensus. Color code publishers and photocopy lessons so everyone can immediately see which materials best match stated objectives. Dissect instructional materials using topic comparisons and horizontal and vertical traces for initial screening and Kid-Ratings for in-depth evaluation. Negotiate with publishers when the competition is most strong for service, materials, and replacement or rebinding. Have stated procedures and photocopied evidence that procedures were followed to avoid court challenges. Finally, provide a system for monitoring and modifying to ensure selected materials will work best for you. Given use of this procedure, your instructional materials will work for you and for your students.

References

American Association of School Librarians and the Association for Educational Communications and Technology. (1991). *Information power: Guidelines for school library media programs*. Washington, DC: Author.

Muther, C. T. (1992). *Textbook adoption: A process for decision-making*. Manchester, CT: Textbook Adoption Advisory Services.

5

Assuring a Safe and Orderly School Environment

If U.S. educators were to publish an official "Constitutional Set of School Guarantees for Students," leading the list of those guarantees would surely be the "Establishment and Maintenance of Safety, Security, and Orderliness Within All Schools and Upon All Playgrounds and Campuses" in our country. The quality of your school is only as good as the perceptions of the community say it is. Much of that perception is drawn from evidence the public gathers in deciding whether or not the school is a place of safety, security, and positive surroundings for students.

The building's physical condition, level of violence, the attitude of students, and neighborhood opinions of local schools are pow-

Assuring a Safe and Orderly Environment 97

erful first impressions made on school visitors. Schools that are unsafe, threatening, and demoralizing institutions have rung national alarm bells during the past two decades. People demand and deserve safe and orderly schools.

5.1 Issues in Creating Safe and Secure Schools

Issues at stake in school safety are centered on the well-being of pupils but also include adequacy of resources and managerial effectiveness of administrators and staff. This chapter will address six areas in designing safe, secure, and orderly schools:

(a) fair disciplinary codes and supporting procedures,
(b) reward and recognition systems,
(c) building and grounds' safety and conditions,
(d) school morale and social supports for students,
(e) up-to-date exemplars of safe and orderly schools, and
(f) administrative actions effecting school safety and orderliness.

This chapter provides you with "how-to" information and suggestions on thinking and talking about safe and orderly schools.

The lists of "indicators" accompanying the discussion of each problem area provide you with an easy way to see how many factors of safety are already present or missing in your school. The "Administrative Actions" lists can be used as self-monitoring tools to assess what you can do to cause improvement in the safety, security, and orderliness of a building. To amplify the usefulness of these lists even more, you may enlist your professional and support staffs (or a random sample) to complete the questionnaires. By comparing your self-reports with those completed by the staff, any discrepancies will be evident. If some do show up, you have an excellent beginning for improving school safety and for building a core of professional resources for team collaboration.

5.2 Overview: The Research and Rationale for Safe Schools

During the 1970s and 1980s, the highly published research on effective schools identified "safe and orderly school environment" as one of the major marks distinguishing the best schools (Squires, Huitt, & Segars, 1985). Along with "high expectations," "strong leadership," and "clear and focused mission," a safe and orderly environment complements the framework of constructing the best possible setting for students (Squires et al., 1985). In addition to the effectiveness research, the comprehensive study, *Violent Schools, Safe Schools: The Safe School Study Report to the Congress* (1978) conducted by the U.S. Department of Health, Education and Welfare, yielded significant findings that expanded educators' notions of "school safety." Findings suggested that, when schools fail or succeed, the reasons are to be found in the following areas: systematic school discipline, adequacy of the reward structure, physical condition of the facility, and the school climate of the students and staff.

The following four problem areas give focus to administrators' efforts to improve safety and security in schools.

A. *Inconsistent Schoolwide Disciplinary Enforcement of Rules*

Most teachers and administrators intuitively know the inherent relationship of sound disciplinary policies and procedures to overall school excellence. The real problem, therefore, in most schools is not: "Should we have rules?" but: "How can we *agree* on what or what not students may do, and how should we *consistently enforce* those agreed-upon rules and regulations?" The first step for administrators is to begin to work toward organizational consensus on specific standards and procedures for the uniform enforcement of policies and regulations by all teachers. Achieving consensus and consistency among the staff on rules and procedural enforcement is more than 90% of the battle. This commitment of staff is necessary, and administrators must receive a "yes" to all of the following:

1. Have teachers and administrators reached consensus on what is acceptable behavior for students?
2. Do students see agreement and consistency among the faculty in the enforcement of school and classroom rules?
3. Do students perceive fairness in the administration of discipline?

Figures 5.1 and 5.2 provide examples of "indicators" and "administrative actions" for gaining schoolwide consistency in discipline.

B. *Ineffective Student Reward and Recognition Systems*

Another obstacle to creating safe and orderly schools is the lack of equitable distribution of rewards to students. To illustrate this point, you can make a quick check on the current condition of the reward system by just walking into any school and gathering evidence to answer the following:

- Which and how many students receive awards?
- How many types of recognition are given to students?
- How many incidents of vandalism and/or property loss are reported?
- What percentage of students receive grades of "A" and "B"?

The Safe School Study (1978) discovered that levels of violence, vandalism, and property loss, as well as motivation for achieving good grades, all have a relationship to the school's form of reward structure. The way students perceive the abundance or scarcity of rewards in a school shapes their feelings of fairness about the system or their anger and frustration about not being successful in it.

Strong competition for a limited number of high grades necessarily filters out many students from being honored and

> (Check [√] the category that applies.)
>
> Yes Some No
>
> 1. ☐ ☐ ☐ Schoolwide rules and regulations are developed and in operation.
>
> 2. ☐ ☐ ☐ All staff are represented in the disciplinary policy development.
>
> 3. ☐ ☐ ☐ Rules are posted, taught, and enforced by all staff.
>
> 4. ☐ ☐ ☐ Students and parents know the discipline policy.
>
> 5. ☐ ☐ ☐ Rules and policy are regularly reviewed by staff.
>
> 6. ☐ ☐ ☐ Racial and gender equity issues are addressed in administering discipline policy.
>
> 7. ☐ ☐ ☐ Due process for students is adhered to by staff.
>
> 8. ☐ ☐ ☐ Teachers use appropriate referral services for problem students.
>
> 9. ☐ ☐ ☐ Students perceive the discipline procedures as "fair."

Figure 5.1. Indicators of Consistency in Schoolwide Discipline

acknowledged. When competition is the dominant form leading to recognition, it can result in students feeling alienated and resentful of the authority figures who pass out the medals and awards. Thus reward structures have serious implications for the sense of security, belongingness, and emotional well-being experienced by students in our schools.

Successful schools devise and frequently revise diverse means of recognition for a broad scope of student performance. Extracurricular activities, for example, provide the less academic students with avenues to excel and to receive accolades. A variety of student activities, such as civic responsibility, coopera-

Assuring a Safe and Orderly Environment 101

(Check [√] the items that apply.)

1. ☐ Facilitate consensus-building processes for staff consistency in disciplinary policy development and enforcement.

2. ☐ Support staff in the appropriate application of disciplinary policy.

3. ☐ Ensure the alignment of school policy and district policy on discipline.

4. ☐ Provide staff development for teachers in due process and classroom management.

5. ☐ Periodically survey students and parents on "fairness" of policy.

6. ☐ Ensure that punishments focus on student misbehavior and avoid humiliation.

7. ☐ Monitor staff for consistency in discipline enforcement.

Figure 5.2. Administrative Actions to Foster Schoolwide Consistency in Discipline

tive attitudes, and community service, are also acknowledged and applauded in effective schools. Figures 5.3 and 5.4 can give you examples and procedures for improving the reward and recognition systems in your school.

c. *Unrepaired and Unpleasant Facilities and Lack of a Crisis Plan*

The message in a nutshell is this: "Keep the building clean and repaired, maintain emergency and code standards, have a crisis management plan, and have some eye for the aesthetics of a school facility." (Upkeep of buildings is discussed in greater detail in Chapter 6.) These variables visibly influence the factors of safety and security of students. Although most districts provide support services for meeting the repair needs and code

(Check [√] the category that applies.)

Yes Some No

1. ☐ ☐ ☐ All students receive recognition.

2. ☐ ☐ ☐ A variety of rewards are provided, such as certificates, honor rolls, photos, and badges.

3. ☐ ☐ ☐ "Inconspicuous" students are discovered and brought into the recognition program.

4. ☐ ☐ ☐ Racial and gender equity concerns are addressed in the reward system.

5. ☐ ☐ ☐ All teachers participate in the reward and recognition system.

6. ☐ ☐ ☐ Cooperative student behavior is recognized.

7. ☐ ☐ ☐ Competition for few rewards is limited.

Figure 5.3. Indicators of an Effective Reward System

standards, the district's scheduled plan of maintenance and frequently reported delay in filling work orders often frustrate administrators.

Fortunate administrators have custodians who take seriously their responsibility for keeping the building clean and safe and who initiate work requests for repairs and for substandard compliance with codes. If you have a custodian or a crew of support personnel of such high caliber, then you have a gold mine! Nevertheless, administrators are the parties responsible for their school's safety and maintenance. The condition of the building makes a powerful impression on the public and students by signaling an attitude and a "personality." Cleanliness, pleasantness, and the timely repair of buildings sends the message to students and the public: "We care about our students, therefore the schools in our district are sound, safe, and inviting places for our students."

Assuring a Safe and Orderly Environment

(Check [√] the items that apply.)

The administrator

1. ☐ involves staff in developing effective recognition system.
2. ☐ allocates adequate funds for individual and group recognition.
3. ☐ looks for potential relationships between student absenteeism and lack of recognition.
4. ☐ addresses racial and gender equity issues in the reward system.
5. ☐ revises recognition program, as needed.
6. ☐ monitors appropriate enforcement of system.
7. ☐ recognizes staff's contribution to the mission of the school.

Figure 5.4. Administrative Actions for Recognition System

The lists in Figures 5.5, 5.6, and 5.7 are not exhaustive, but they do point to critical areas of safety. The district office plays an important role, as do public health agencies, in setting standards and maintaining the condition of the school building.

D. *Lack of a Cohesive, Supportive School Climate*

Inconsistent enforcement of disciplinary rules and lack of adequate recognition and rewards have been isolated as factors to address in administrative efforts to improve the safety and security of schools. Also, the "climate" of a school has powerful implications related to student unrest, frustration, and alienation. The amount and type of human interaction in schools will shape students' socialization and sense of community. Without cohesive, coherent, and positive interactive climate, students will be shortchanged. Students want fulfillment of their basic

(Check [√] the items that apply.)

1. The building is free from obvious safety hazards and code violations:
   - ☐ electric outlets and switches
   - ☐ fire extinguishers
   - ☐ bell and warning systems
   - ☐ heating and cooling systems
   - ☐ playground equipment
   - ☐ others (specify)

2. The support staff has had in-service on hazardous materials:
   - ☐ asbestos/lead/other

3. The general appearance of the building and grounds is neat, pleasant, and clean:
   - ☐ adequate painting
   - ☐ bathrooms clean and graffiti removed
   - ☐ hallways and floors swept and washed
   - ☐ walls clean and tastefully decorated
   - ☐ handicapped accessible
   - ☐ good lighting

4. ☐ The intercommunications system is adequate and functioning.

5. ☐ Potential problem areas are adequately supervised and locked, if appropriate (i.e., nurses' medication storage cabinet, custodians' solutions, disinfectants' storage, and so on).

6. ☐ Traffic areas are free from safety hazards, such as off-site sidewalks, vehicle entrances and exits to school, student loading areas.

Figure 5.5. Indicators of a Well-Maintained, Repaired Building

---

(Check [√] the items that apply.)

1. A crisis management plan is developed and in operation for
   - ☐ bomb threat procedures
   - ☐ explosion, fire, tornado procedures
   - ☐ evacuation plan
   - ☐ suicide postvention
   - ☐ student death postvention
   - ☐ teacher death postvention
   - ☐ dangerous intruder

2. ☐ A crisis chain of command has been established and communicated to all staff, such as secretarial, administrative, custodial, and teaching.

3. ☐ Student traffic patterns have been established for inside and outside the building.

4. ☐ Parents are aware of where their children will be transported in the event of an evacuation of the building.

5. ☐ Appropriate teams have been designated for roles in a crisis, such as teachers, secretaries, psychologists, and custodial.

Figure 5.6. Crisis Management Plan

needs for belongingness and for a sense of social responsibility. Students must feel connected to a social unit that acknowledges and values their membership.

You can respond to the problem of a divisive or apathetic school climate by incorporating goals and action plans related to school spirit and pupil bonding with the school into your management practices. Figures 5.8 and 5.9 identify examples of how to build a proud and spirited student body.

(Check [√] the items that apply.)

1. ☐ Perform a building audit on the condition of the building. Compile results.

2. ☐ Include the building custodian and other key support personnel in the audit.

3. ☐ Complete and follow-up on all necessary work order forms.

4. ☐ Respond to fire marshal and other safety officials' reports.

5. ☐ Address staff and students on all safety issues.

6. ☐ Respond to parental, staff, and student complaints.

7. ☐ Collect data related to number and types of accidents.

8. ☐ Conduct training and practice for students and staff in emergency procedures.

9. ☐ Designate and provide in-service for crisis management teams.

Figure 5.7. Administrative Actions for Safety and Crisis Management

5.3 Summary

Educators in effective schools recognize that managing an efficient and well-run facility sets the stage for success and excellence in other significant areas of student life. Good schools incorporate within their daily regimen sound discipline and reward systems. Good schools maintain a repaired and decorated building to provide pleasant conditions for students. Good schools are characterized by a climate of cohesiveness and social support for students. Good schools also have routinized referral and communication procedures that truly free pupils to concentrate on learning and behaving. Given these attributes of schools, students will value the knowledge and positive experiences designed for their growth and success.

Assuring a Safe and Orderly Environment 107

(Check [√] the items that apply.)

1. ☐ School conducts periodic climate surveys for staff and students.

2. ☐ School has many indicators of school spirit, such as school song, logo, T-shirts, jackets, clubs, and cooperative assemblies.

3. ☐ Citizenship, service, athletics, academics, and the like are recognized.

4. ☐ "Buddy" mentoring relationships are formally structured for students.

5. ☐ Student due process is adhered to by all staff.

6. ☐ Self-esteem objectives and action plans are part of all teachers' lesson plans and classroom delivery.

7. ☐ Staff models cooperation and cohesiveness among themselves.

8. ☐ "School-within-a-School" units or Advisory Programs personalize the school climate for students.

9. ☐ Absenteeism data are reviewed frequently for potential relationship to student alienation.

10. ☐ Teachers incorporate cooperative learning strategies and self-esteem curriculum within their repertoire of lesson designs and delivery.

11. ☐ Student caring, courtesy, and cooperation are recognized.

Figure 5.8. Indicators of a Cohesive, Positive School Spirit

Exceptional school administrators realize that safety, security, and orderliness do not happen by accident; they are the result of specific administrative competencies and actions that create the best environment for students. Behind the scenes in

> (Check [√] the items that apply.)
>
> 1. ☐ Involve staff in consensus meetings related to increasing school cohesiveness.
>
> 2. ☐ Provide staff in-service in cooperative learning, citizenship development, and self-esteem.
>
> 3. ☐ Establish specific goals and action plans to increase school cohesiveness.
>
> 4. ☐ Collect data from students and staff on school climate.
>
> 5. ☐ Allocate adequate funds for staff development on cooperative learning and related topics.
>
> 6. ☐ Monitor classroom climates and teacher attitudes related to self-esteem needs of students.
>
> 7. ☐ Provide in-service to staff on student due process and hearing procedures.
>
> 8. ☐ Model two-way communication and collaboration with staff members.
>
> 9. ☐ Recognize multicultural and gender equity concerns in the formula for building school cohesiveness.

Figure 5.9. Administrative Actions for Establishing a Cohesive, Positive School Spirit

excellent schools, high-caliber administrative practices are found. Administrators enlist a variety of professional and support resources within and outside of their school to reach their goal of safety and security. These administrators allocate a significant amount of attention to collaboration, consensus building, staff teamwork, and clockwork follow-through in promoting staff-wide agreement and team action. By establishing schoolwide systems and procedures, administrators have minimized (and, in some cases, eradicated) the nuisances, serious obstacles, and threats that plague the school system.

In short, successful schools across the country have assertively addressed safety and security problems and have discovered working solutions. They have identified and developed programs, policies, and procedures that create positive and safe settings for students. Other administrators can do the same for their schools by following their examples.

References

Squires, D. H., Huitt, W. G., & Segars, J. K. (1985). *Effective schools and classrooms: A research-based perspective.* Alexandria, VA: Association of Supervision and Curriculum Development.

U.S. Department of Health, Education and Welfare. (1978). *Violent schools, safe schools: The safe school study to the Congress, executive summary.* Washington, DC: Government Printing Office.

6

Planning, Improving, and Maintaining School Facilities

It is difficult, if not impossible, to separate an activity from the environment in which it occurs. Space, lighting, heating and cooling, acoustics, plumbing, type of floor and wall surfaces, and furnishings can greatly affect what can and cannot be accomplished in a given facility. Moreover, facility requirements change over time. What was adequate in the one-room country school 50 years ago is not adequate in our technology-laden schools today.

6.1 Facilities and Educational Quality

Effective became a popular word in school circles in the 1980s, springing from research on factors contributing to the quality of schooling. Some of these factors have implications for educational facilities and school environments. School administrators need to be aware of the factors that have been found to be highly helpful to promoting effectiveness in schools. In addition, school facilities must be evaluated carefully with an eye toward maximizing effectiveness.

Some selected indicators of quality, or effectiveness, that are germane to facility services include

(a) a safe, orderly environment conducive to teaching and learning (Lezotte, 1983);
(b) order and a businesslike atmosphere in the school (Larkin, 1984);
(c) safe, clean, and adequate physical facilities (Larkin, 1984); and
(d) school site management and district support (Purkey & Smith, 1983; 1985).

It is easy to see that the environmental contexts of schooling are important factors in the success of teaching and learning. Given suitable facilities and environments, teaching and learning may thrive.

6.2 Facilities Management

Any school administrator is likely to have a vision of the ideal place for learning. The vision and the reality, however, are often quite different things. The challenge is to get the reality of the school congruent with the ideal vision of a place for learning. Ideally, a school campus should be a harmonized environment that allows for maximum efficiency in learning and operational processes while maintaining a pleasant, attractive atmosphere in which pupils, personnel, and patrons can achieve success and satisfaction.

6.3 Evaluating School Facilities

The tangible characteristics of a school facility contribute to or detract from the quality of the instructional program. You, as the administrator, have the responsibility to determine the status of and the interrelationships between facility and program. Steps in fulfilling this responsibility include many of the factors outlined below.

A. *Function*

In the best of worlds, your school's form, or facility, would follow function, or program. Therefore before you can evaluate your facility, you must first determine its function. Conceptualization of the instructional program's mission, goals, objectives, and intended outcomes must come ahead of any determination of a facility's form or design adequacy. Once you know what it is you want to do, then you can see whether your facilities are suitable to get done what you want to do. Guidance for this task is available in the current literature (Kaufman, 1991).

B. *Impact*

Once the school's purposes and outcomes are clearly defined, you must then determine the extent to which those outcomes are influenced by the facilities you have. Sometimes the facility dictates the program, rather than the other way around. With comprehensive staff and patron participation, identify specific ways in which the facility constrains, enhances, or otherwise influences the programs and services you wish to implement. Examples of things that affect use include energy conservation, power availability, handicapped access, and other special requirements. Configuration also affects use. For example, the cafeteria could be designed with a separate lock system allowing entrance but precluding access to other areas of the school. Flexibility under these circumstances enables convenient public use of the cafeteria without disruption of other spaces.

c. Adequacy

Three major elements affect adequacy: enrollment, space availability, and space use. Enrollment in schools across the nation never seems to stand still. It is either going up or going down. You need to determine accurately which way it is going for your school for the next five years or so. Dependable enrollment projection is accomplished in several ways (Kowalski, 1983).

Determining space availability involves a careful inventory. What space do you have in your school? Note space sizes, ventilation, floor surfaces, lighting, occupancy capacity limits, access, safety, hazards, and potential uses. All space should be listed and characteristics should be tabulated. This gives you an accurate definition of what space exists or what may be used given reasonable conditions.

Space use is a product of several factors. Factors used in determining use might focus on location, spatial relationships, energy components, sound or visual components, aesthetics, maintenance requirements, time of use, and other factors. Time of use is usually calculated with use of a building-use chart, in which each room or space is listed, along with its rated capacity and the number of occupants on an hourly basis. The school's time schedule may be used as the hourly units, and time should be monitored during all possible ranges (e.g., 6 a.m. to 10 p.m.). Community uses should also be factored into calculation of building use. For example, if the cafeteria is used by a senior citizen square dancing group on Tuesday evenings, or if the auditorium is rented by a local church on Sunday morning, such use should be included in the calculation.

D. Appraisal

Appraisal calls for your judgment of the facility's educational and structural suitability in accordance with your findings on function, impact, and adequacy. Generally, the findings would indicate whether or not the facility is adequate or inadequate in quality and quantity to fulfill its function or to enable accomplishment of the school's mission. If the facility is inadequate in quality, then renovation, modification, or disposal may be required. If it is inadequate in quantity of space, construction or expansion might be needed.

Understanding the comprehensive characteristics of a school facility is critical to determining its suitability to deliver the intended functions of the school. Moreover, it is essential to ascertaining your needs for the future.

6.4 Facility Planning

Given a carefully determined evaluation of facilities, new or reconditioned space may be required. You may then find it appropriate to move ahead following the key steps and procedures outlined below. Any proposed facility should be an outgrowth of three factors: (a) your facility evaluation, above; (b) an assessment of your financial resources; and (c) your facility planning requisites.

A. Educational Specifications

Before structural and construction design can begin, the school administrator must involve the potential users and constituents of the proposed facility in the development of written conceptual ingredients. These ingredients are set forth as educational specifications, which include a description of the facility's occupants and clientele, the programs and services to be housed, and the proposed workings and uses of space. Educational specifications usually are not precise descriptions of an instructional program. You must provide enough information, however, so architects can translate your educational objectives and operational needs into technical designs to direct construction.

Purpose. The proposed purpose of the facility, its justification, and its general uses must be outlined to give the designers a conceptualization of the nature of the project. Information about the community characteristics germane to the project should be included as well as the source of funding.

Components. All curricular, extracurricular, specialized, administrative, service, and community programs and services to be housed in the facility must be clearly defined in operational and goal-oriented terms. Type of pupil clientele, instructional methodologies and strategies used, and goals of learning activities should also be defined. Characteristics of each activity must be clearly drawn for interpretation by the architect into building design. Further, the scope and sequence of all curriculum activities to be carried out in the school must be explained and described as well as the range, number, size, and type of spaces desired. Issues of security, flexibility, and general utility must also be described in terms of applicability to facility planning.

Relationships. Relationships between personnel, activities, programs, services, and spaces must be clearly defined for the building designer. Identifying the intended interrelationships of building spaces gives direction for configuring locations and proximities by the architect. You should also include any flexibility considerations, circulation requirements, community or special access requirements, and communication needs as a part of your specifications.

Quality, quantity, and cost. You should provide a listing of the net square footage desired in the building as well as a description of the general features that comprise quality or value. Types of materials desired, numbers of students and staff, number of spaces desired, and any special features (i.e., skylights, utilities, or environmental conditions) must be contained in the educational specifications. It's important for you to remember that quality, quantity, and cost are interrelated variables. If cost is constant, quantity is inversely proportional to quality. In other words, trying to get more quantity of space while holding cost constant will reduce the quality, or value, of your facility.

B. *Design Services*

Some administrators decide to employ professional architectural services early in the planning process, and many architects are highly skilled in working with groups in this way. Basically, the architect can provide you with several levels of service, which are listed below.

Predesign planning. Design begins after several predesign matters have been resolved. These include establishing the need for the project, obtaining policy-level approval, securing funding, selecting a site, and preparing educational specifications. It is helpful, and often advisable, to use architects in many of these predesign activities. Professional architects or engineers may facilitate the success of a project with advisory services at all levels of planning. As the coordinating administrator, you are likely to find that such professional advice is invaluable throughout the project.

Schematic design. In this phase, the architect takes the educational specifications and begins to configure concepts and designs that implement the educators' wishes. You should expect to work closely with the architect in this phase, which results in a set of line drawings of the whole facility. After approval by the governing board, the basic building design is set, and the exterior design is conceptually established for the remainder of the project.

Design development. The next phase of design is development and refinement of drawings for construction of the facility by the architectural firm. The design is polished, and the facility and landscape design and construction characteristics are fully developed. The administrator must remain in close contact and consult frequently with the architect during this phase.

Construction documents. The construction documents are prepared by the architect and include a complete set of working drawings and a set of construction specifications. The working drawings comprise a series of drawings that illustrate and define the specific nature of the project design and all components included. The technical specifications document is a comprehensive collection of detailed information about materials and equipment to be used, standards of construction workmanship, and contractual documents for bidding and contractual relationships. You, as the administrator, must coordinate any specific equipment requirements or other special needs of your school district with the architect in the preparation of the construction documents.

Bidding process. In the bidding process, you can count on the architect to provide many services including preparing bid advertisements and announcements, issuing construction document sets to prospective bidders, processing inquiries about the project during the bid phase, opening and evaluating bids submitted by contractors, and assisting your legal counsel in the preparation of documents.

Construction supervision. The architect can assist you greatly in the construction phase of the project. As your representative, the architect should make regular inspection visits to the construction site (preferably daily) to ensure proper work and materials and to advise you as to approval for payments to be made to the contractor. The architect should be the authority as to what the construction documents intend, should prepare any necessary change orders for your approval, and should serve as the liaison between you and the contractor.

c. Other Considerations

Some administrators have hired professional construction managers to assure increased supervision of compliance with construction documents. Other professional services needed may include site selection assistance, cost-benefit studies, interior design and furnishings selection, and postoccupancy evaluation services.

6.5 Selecting an Architect

One of the toughest things an educational administrator has to do is to select a provider of purchased professional services, including architects. In finding an architect, it's advisable for you to follow the guidelines set forth in the list below.

Selection of an architect rarely involves design competition, except for very large projects. In design competition, architects submit alternative solutions to a design project, and the school administration judges the submissions to select the desired firm. After selection, the decision to employ an architect is formalized by action of the governing board, and you have an obligation to supply the board with sufficient information to make a sound decision. Using a well-designed selection process helps fulfill that obligation.

Comparative Process

1. Obtain expressions of interest from firms (including information on years in practice, areas of specialization, and past clients).
2. Narrow down the list to six to ten qualified firms and issue a request for proposals (include project budget, time schedule, preliminary design program, and desired range and nature of services to be provided). Do not include fees at this point.
3. Receive written proposals from firms and evaluate them on the basis of budget compliance, schedule capabilities, project team, and documented performance.

Planning and Maintaining Facilities

4. Select only three to four firms for final interview—no more, not even for "courtesy" purposes.
5. Interview each firm for not less than one hour in separate rooms. The architect sets up in an assigned room, and the interview team comes in at an appointed time for the interview. This prevents the confusion of set up and take down between interviews.
6. Evaluate firms on demonstrated ability for creative problem solving, individual ideas and solutions, and organizational integrity.
7. Select the best firm and negotiate agreement on fees and contract provisions. Do not use the architect's contract format, usually supplied by the American Institute of Architects. For your own protection, let your legal counsel advise you on what you want in your contract with your architect.
8. Sign the contract, obtain necessary approvals, and begin the project.

6.6 Stewardship and Care of Facilities and Resources

The appearance and cleanliness of a building give you a quick surface perspective on how well a building is being maintained. Appearance may be a telling indicator of the quality of care a building is receiving. If a building is dirty and unkempt, it is likely to be in poor working order or in need of repair or attention. Your job as administrator is to set standards for care and upkeep of facilities and resources, to assign staff to perform the responsibilities, to provide staff with necessary equipment and supplies to do the job, and to inspect regularly to evaluate the quality of maintenance. This section will describe how you can fulfill these responsibilities.

A. *Custodial Services*

There is more to custodial services than just vacuuming, sweeping, and washing surfaces. School facilities must be cleaned in all aspects, but they also must be protected, maintained, repaired, environmentally regulated, operated, and supportive of their educational purposes. Sound programs of custodial services can assure better performance of educational purposes. Administrative responsibility for delivery of sound custodial services is crucial in successful operation of the school.

B. *Administrative Responsibilities*

Primary responsibilities include identification of mode of services, selection of personnel, staff development of custodial staff, preventive maintenance planning, work supervision, and energy management.

Mode of services. Most school districts employ their own custodial staff and maintenance program personnel. The use of external, or contract, providers of services, however, has been growing steadily in many parts of the country. Contracted services, sometimes referred to as "privatization," have many advantages and disadvantages, as does self-employment for services. The following delineation of administrative tasks assumes a program of self-employment; however, a more detailed discussion of privatization can be found at the end of the chapter.

Selection of custodians. Two areas you should consider when selecting custodians are these: How many personnel are needed for the space you have? What characteristics should you look for in hiring custodial personnel?

Custodial staffing adequacy. Many techniques have been employed to prescribe the number of custodians needed—number of students, square footage of space, numbers of individual rooms, nature of facilities, and number of faculty—to name a few. There is no magic formula. Custodial work load factors depend upon the type of facility (athletic locker room versus history classroom), site location (urban city versus rural country), educational program (computerized chemistry versus kindergarten), climate (sweltering southwest versus frigid north central), complexities (large rest room versus narrow hallway), quality and quantity of equipment (mop and bucket versus automatic waxing machine), and labor practices (contractual limitations). Other factors affect staffing levels as well, but perhaps a good rule of thumb is planning on between 2,000 and 3,000 square feet per man-hour of work to yield acceptable levels of performance, depending on many of the variables above (Association of School Business Officials, 1981).

Custodial hiring considerations. Custodial services should consist of qualified people who are properly prepared, equipped, and trained to do their job. To assure satisfactory hiring results, you must take care to select high-caliber, efficient personnel who can get the job done and get it done right. Key qualifications include dependability and good work habits, ability to work and relate effectively with people (young ones, especially), willingness to learn, reliability and trustworthiness, unblemished ethical character, and adequate academic and vocational skills. The custodian's job is a major responsibility, and a good custodian can keep a school shipshape and make it hum with verve and esprit.

Staff development. It's not enough to hire good people and then let them take off on their own to do the job. You must orient the new employee to the job and provide training on requirements and standards of the work, conditions of acceptable performance, proper use of tools and materials, work schedules (including breaks and meals), school rules and regulations, student and staff relations and responsibilities, and other work operations. Just as it's reasonable to provide regular, systematic training for faculty and staff to achieve excellence, it's just as reasonable to see to the custodian's orientation and training for excellence.

c. *Preventative Maintenance*

To extend the life of everything in the school (even including people), efforts must be taken regularly to protect, preserve, and keep the school and its contents in good working order. A program of maintenance should be developed that identifies items and systems, specifies the standards of operation or conditions, provides direction for action to be taken, and establishes a regular schedule for such action. For example, the heating and cooling system must have clean air circulating through its coils and vents, and filters must be changed every month or so to meet this requirement. A filter, worth pocket change, is a critical element in a very expensive system. By establishing a program of maintenance, systems and equipment will not break down or fail, and your school can function well and in healthy condition.

D. *Work Supervision*

A seasoned administrator once remarked, "What is inspected is what is respected." Whether or not this is true, you have a duty to provide oversight and appraisal of every aspect of work performed under your supervision. Supervision of maintenance involves planning, participation, procedures, and follow-up. Plans should be made as to what will be inspected and how it will be checked. Key staff must participate in the development and implementation of such plans. Procedures must be established that outline all expectations and functions, including how feedback will be obtained. In addition, evaluation results must produce action—perhaps reinforcement for good performance or direction for any needed improvement. Given appropriate supervision on your part, staff and systems can operate at appropriate levels and keep your school running up to par. An example of a classroom inspection checklist is provided in Figure 6.1.

6.7 Energy Management

Some school districts are fortunate enough to have computerized energy management systems, which monitor the consumption of energy in a given facility. These systems are invaluable in holding down costs due to energy use. Until you have such a

Planning and Maintaining Facilities 123

School: _____	Classroom: _____
Inspected by: _____	Date: _____

Area	Condition	Comments
	Acceptable Not Acceptable	
Bulletin and chalkboards	☐ ☐ ☐	_____
	Acceptable Not Acceptable	
Cabinets and hardware	☐ ☐ ☐	_____
	Acceptable Not Acceptable	
Ceiling and lights	☐ ☐ ☐	_____
	Acceptable Not Acceptable	
Equipment and materials	☐ ☐ ☐	_____
	Acceptable Not Acceptable	
Floors or carpet	☐ ☐ ☐	_____
	Acceptable Not Acceptable	
Furniture and bookcases	☐ ☐ ☐	_____
	Acceptable Not Acceptable	
HVAC and duct work	☐ ☐ ☐	_____
	Acceptable Not Acceptable	
Shades or blinds	☐ ☐ ☐	_____
	Acceptable Not Acceptable	
Sinks and plumbing fixtures	☐ ☐ ☐	_____
	Acceptable Not Acceptable	
Storage and lockers	☐ ☐ ☐	_____
	Acceptable Not Acceptable	
Walls and trim	☐ ☐ ☐	_____
	Acceptable Not Acceptable	
Windows and glass	☐ ☐ ☐	_____

Figure 6.1. Classroom Inspection Checklist
NOTE: The three boxes indicate the range of possible conditions from "Acceptable" to "Not Acceptable".

system in place, or even if you do have such a system, however, custodians are key persons in conservation and economical operation of energy-using systems in your school. As a part of the work requirements, specific duties for the custodian should include monitoring thermostats, water heating systems, insulation, electrical and plumbing fixtures, and mechanical systems. The custodian is an effective agent for gathering important feedback about the consumption of energy. A dollar spent needlessly on energy consumption is a dollar that cannot be spent on teaching and learning.

6.8 Summary

Educational facilities must be planned and provided for in accordance with our best knowledge about how teaching and learning can best be effectuated. We know that the environment for education is a part of education. Once the space is acquired and provided, the conscientious administrator has many responsibilities to assure that the facilities continue to be maintained and supportive of the educational program.

References

Association of School Business Officials (ASBO) International. (1981). *Custodial methods and procedures manual.* Reston, VA: Author.
Council of Educational Facility Planners International. (1982). *Guide for planning educational facilities.* Columbus, OH: Author.
Kaufman, R. (1992). *Strategic thinking and planning in education.* Newbury Park, CA: Sage.
Kowalski, T. J. (1983). *Solving educational facility problems.* Muncie, IN: Accelerated Development Inc.
Larkin, R. F. (1984). Achievement directed leadership. *The Effective School Report, 2,* 3.
Lezotte, L. W. (1983). The five correlates of an effective school. *The Effective School Report, 1,* 3-4.
Purkey, S. C., & Smith, M. S. (1983). Effective schools: A review. *The Elementary School Journal, 83,* 427-452.
Purkey, S. C., & Smith, M. S. (1985). School reform: The district policy implications of the effective school literature. *The Elementary School Journal, 85,* 353-389.

7

Broadening Computer Technology Functions for Quality Schools

Computers and other types of technology have become important implements in the management and functioning of schools. With good planning, a school administrator can contribute significantly to the efficiency and productivity of any school system through the use of technology. Depending primarily upon how well you plan and select uses and applications, adding technology to a school organization may be a positive force in advancing effectiveness.

Many administrators already have a significant number of computers in their schools and will be adding more hardware to their technology arsenal as time and resources permit. Others have yet to bring their first computer into their office or school.

In either situation, the information in this chapter will be helpful for fostering an understanding of how to introduce computers and other forms of technology into the school environment in a sensible way.

The chapter includes discussions of applications, programs, and services available to the school administrator from computer technology. Software selection and hardware layouts are offered for small, medium, and large school systems. Ways of planning for computer technology systems for use in school operations are provided, which may help you to improve teaching, learning, and school operations. This chapter is by no means a complete guide for introducing technology into any school, but it gives you a starting point for planning and discussing some of the relevant issues.

7.1 Uses of Computer Technology in Schools

Technology becomes a useful educational and managerial tool when it is used to execute the appropriate functions. Recent uses in computer technology in school programs and services have included the following:

Custom-designed applications
Data base management
Desktop publishing
Enrollment forecasting
Event and school scheduling
Graphics and presentations
Inventory control
On-line information access
Records management
Spreadsheets and accounting
Statistical analyses
Telecommunications
Transportation scheduling
Word processing

Computer Technology Functions 127

The range of uses of computers in school administration seems almost limitless. Today's principal is likely to perform the following activities during a typical day with the computer: check the electronic log to see how many parents were called the previous evening by a computer-operated attendance reporting system, edit and laser-print several letters prepared by the school secretary complete with custom school letterhead, draft the format for a three-column informational brochure aimed at parents, log onto the district mainframe to check for incoming electronic mail, send several electronic mail messages to the central office and to other principals, query the data base for the home addresses and phone numbers of students referred to the office, transmit a supply order to a vendor by computer fax, prepare a personalized note to several teachers with mail-merge, add several requests to the school's budget spreadsheet for the coming year, use a computer modem to check with an airline guide service for airfares to an upcoming convention, and verify current unencumbered balances in the budget of a school department requesting a purchase order.

Not every administrator wants to use all of the capabilities a computer offers. It is helpful to know just what computer technology provides, however, so you can select functions and services germane to your own needs. To see how you might compare with other educational computer users, try completing the survey questionnaire in Table 7.1.

7.2 Major Application Program Options

There are basically two options for obtaining applications and programs to meet your school needs: (a) purchase complete off-the-shelf program products and (b) develop custom-programmed applications. Custom-programmed applications may be needed for certain uses such as meeting complex accounting or student information system requirements. Such products are expensive, however, and usually developed to very narrow specifications defined by a particular set of circumstances.

TABLE 7.1 Computer Checklist: Your School's CQ (Computer Quotient)

Directions: Check the functions and services provided by computer technology in your school district. Add up your score at the end to see how your school measures up.

Our school uses computers for

- ☐ scheduling pupils and classes
- ☐ teacher development of learner materials
- ☐ shopping for airline fares and travel accommodations
- ☐ teleconferencing with homebound pupils
- ☐ ordering merchandise from vendors
- ☐ reinforcing basic skills in high-priority content areas
- ☐ statistically monitoring school demographics
- ☐ teaching students keyboarding skills by third grade
- ☐ accessing and downloading files from on-line data bases
- ☐ supplementing conventional instruction in interest centers accessible to pupils
- ☐ school-level budget development
- ☐ teaching students programming in BASIC or more advanced languages
- ☐ electronic mail with other schools and departments
- ☐ in-service training activities and staff development
- ☐ word processing for office correspondence
- ☐ ensuring all students are proficient in computer use by sixth grade
- ☐ school-level fiscal accounting and monitoring of accounts
- ☐ producing the school newspaper or newsletter with graphics and computer art
- ☐ individualizing mailings to large groups of people with print-merge processes
- ☐ teaching creative writing
- ☐ designing and maintaining student records
- ☐ decreasing student absenteeism with automatic voice parent notification system
- ☐ identifying pupils for meal charges (with bar codes or other automatic data entry)
- ☐ providing for the special needs of unique students and students at risk

Computer Technology Functions

TABLE 7.1 (continued)

- ☐ monitoring teacher distributions of grades among students and classes
- ☐ routing school buses and scheduling pupil pickup stops
- ☐ obtaining technical advice from on-line computer technical services
- ☐ conducting a cost-effectiveness analysis of program alternatives
- ☐ maintaining the school's master calendar
- ☐ inventory control and equipment management

- ☐ teaching pupils creative programming with LOGO
- ☐ providing students with access to career and college information systems
- ☐ computer-assisted instruction for delivery of whole courses
- ☐ enabling teachers to do class preparation and planning off site (check out or modem)
- ☐ charting student assessment information for disaggregation
- ☐ checking library and media in and out (with bar codes or other automatic data entry)

Scoring: Count the applications and services you checked in each column. Compare your score to the following chart to see how your school stacks up:

Score	Left Column (management)	Right Column (instruction)
15 or more	Highly advanced management user	Way out front in instructional uses
10-14	First-class use of management tools	High marks in instructional applications
5-9	Management helped with technology	Instruction boosted by technology
4 or Less	Lack of tools makes management suffer	Pupils may miss the information age

Off-the-shelf programs are commonly used and sufficient for most requirements in schools. Most applications are an implementation or combination of seven categorical divisions:

(a) instructional support and assistance;
(b) word processing and desktop publishing;
(c) spreadsheets and accounting;
(d) data base management;
(e) graphics, painting, and drawing;
(f) communications; and
(g) program or application development.

There are many commercial programs available that are forms of these seven basic functions, resulting in instructional and management tools that are more flexible than paper and pencil. What administrators need to know for their school is addressed in the discussion of each of the seven categories that follows.

7.3 Instructional Support and Assistance

Teaching and learning can be greatly enhanced by many educational programs and applications available from software dealers and educational agencies. Much of the software of this type is obtainable in a variety of operating system formats, compatible with popular computers, in both academic and practical curricular areas. In addition, these educational distributors and commercial vendors are developing and offering greater numbers of programs and applications all the time.

Instructional applications. Examples of instructional computer programs currently on the market include the following:

On-line data bases for access   (Mindscape)
to meteorological information
from around the world

Computer Technology Functions

Study aids for college entrance examinations with sample questions and answers	(Studyware)
Tutor-type program to learn keyboarding with speed and accuracy	(Simon & Schuster)
Vocabulary development programs that teach vowel and word sounds	(MECC)
Basic arithmetic programs with applied practice activities	(MECC)
Programs to teach writing and storytelling with language structure	(IBM, MECC)
Historical analysis of life on the American frontier	(MECC)
Games to teach addition, subtraction, and number relationships	(The Learning Co.)
Sentence and story learning activities in game form	(The Learning Co.)
Foreign language word and phrase drills with voice augmentation	(Penton Overseas)
Geographic and demographic data in a map and reference library	(Software Toolworks)
Electronic editions of encyclopedia-like libraries	(Random House, Grolier)

Extensive instructional materials are available for use with school computers, and the number of options is growing steadily. Given appropriate planning and selection, curriculum content also can be augmented with computer programs. In addition, conventional instruction can be supplemented with "patient" machines that persevere indefinitely (until the power is turned off) in reinforcing basic skills for students. More advanced applications are available for higher-order learning.

On-line information services. An immense amount of information is available to students through computerized information retrieval systems and on-line data bases. With on-line (or terminal access by phone or direct line) services, students can communicate with a remote computer system to access news, scientific information, business market data, commentary, current and historical information, advice on hundreds of topics, on-line games, electronic clubs and discussion forums, and research and reference services. More information is provided in the section on communications below.

Higher-order learning. Computers are a powerful aid in higher-order learning processes in several ways. First, the ease and speed of access to information allows extensive and comprehensive research by bringing the data to the student. Second, computers can handle repetitive tasks and routine steps in student inquiries with macros (preset computer action templates), "if-then" hypothesis testing programs, and the student-generated applications mentioned above. Third, students can work cooperatively on projects with others who may be thousands of miles away, while the computer keeps track of their activities and outcomes so groups can easily build on each other's work. Finally, simulations allow students to try new and unconventional ideas out without risk or embarrassment.

Making use of this problem-solving environment is one of the great advantages for students in the development of their learning and intellectual growth. The student who has a computer and knows how to use it has significant advantages in instructional delivery. Computer-aided instruction (CAI) is a cost-effective and powerful avenue to higher-order cognitive and interdisciplinary skills.

Students can use the computer to produce creative work with text, graphics, and data. Moreover, with hypermedia (combining text, graphics, video, and sound) application generators like

Linkway (IBM) or *Toolbook* (Asymetrix), both DOS-based systems, or *Hypercard* (Apple Macintosh), students can solve or develop solutions for problems by writing their own applications. Object-oriented, easy-to-use programming language allows the student to create the most advanced, graphics-rich applications that link associated ideas for complex tasks and functions. Students can retrieve and link complex pieces of information using an index card-like system.

There are several packages now available for computers that can be used to build applications using hypermedia links as the glue for traditional text-to-text linking. These applications allow students to jump between related bits of information regardless of location. For example, a student might link some geographic information about Japan from a word processing program, with a map of Japan produced by a cartographic program, and with pictures of Japan found in an electronic encyclopedia. The entire production can be media produced by a presentation graphics package for publication, for addition to the school's media collection, or for a group presentation.

A. *Selecting Software for Instructional Delivery*

Schools should not turn curriculum development and instructional design over to computer technology any more than they should turn it over to textbook publishers. Truly integrated computer-based learning systems must be developed by schools in response to assessed and identified needs of learners. Today's off-the-shelf programs have much to offer, but they lack flexibility to meet the diverse and complex learning needs of students. As supplemental tools, however, computers provide well-constructed, ably configured instructional systems that have value in the learning process. Because they can be very useful, by augmenting quality teaching extremely well, there is a vital role for them in the delivery of the school's curriculum.

How does the administrator with limited software and computer experience properly evaluate instructional software? Actually, the process is similar to that for the evaluation and selection of other learning materials (see Chapter 4). Some of the unique factors the administrator must consider are listed below.

(1) Method. The specific methodology of the software design must be identified and judged for suitability. What is the intended activity for the software? Is it for drill and practice? Tutorial instruction? Simulation for problem solving? Games for reinforcement or entertainment? Enrichment or remediation?

(2) Content. Learning tasks must be appropriate to help learners meet their objectives. Does the program have specific objectives? Is the content accurate? Is it appropriate? Does it support the school's curriculum? What knowledge or skills must the student possess to use it? Is the required ability level suitable or flexible?

(3) Design. The application must measure up to established standards of instructional practice and design. Does the software meet developmental needs of the learner (grade level, age, ability)? Does the program adhere to fundamental principles of teaching and learning? Is it logically organized? Who is in control—the student or the computer? Does the program permit looping back for repetition or exit at any point? Is the program motivating and appealing? Does the program maintain records of student progress for teacher use?

(4) Operation. Technical aspects of the software's construction must be sound, affordable, and easy to use. Does the program make full use of the computer? Are instructions clear to students? Can the program be interrupted or entered at any point? Is it grammatically sound and free of bias? Are the command codes or access easy to use? What is the life expectancy of the program? Are the operating instructions thorough and easy to understand? Are screen layout and design proper?

Administrators can select instructional software even with limited knowledge of computers. Technology, like any other instructional tool, must be evaluated for suitability for use in an effective program of teaching and learning. Although the task may be new to the administrator, it is one that must be mastered to keep up with advances in instructional technology.

7.4 Word Processing and Desktop Publishing

Word processing programs and applications permit educators to produce nearly any kind of written document. Today's word processing programs are easy to use, provide a wide range of capabilities, and can generate a limitless number of documents. The better word processing programs are self-instructional and include on-line help and assistance to the user. Text material can be integrated with graphics and numerical data, and these same programs permit wide variety in formatting documents. Preparation of correspondence, memoranda, manuscripts, publications, forms, and other documents is a standard use of word processing programs. Basic capabilities found in even the simplest word processing programs include inserting, deleting, changing, and moving typed text. Moving text from one document to another is possible, even from other programs and computer systems. For example, Apple Macintosh documents can easily be translated to IBM DOS-based formats in seconds, and vice versa.

A. *Selecting a Word Processing Program*

In selecting a word processing program, features are an important consideration. Some of the popular and useful options include spell checking, thesaurus and dictionary support, grammar checking, diverse fonts and type sizes, and automatic tables of contents, indexes, and page numbering. Transfer of numbers, text, and pictures from other programs directly into the application is another useful capability. Integrated file conversion is handy, as are print previewing, style templates, macros, and table construction options. Good word processing programs permit data sharing with other programs, document templates, customized menus, diversified formatting, very long documents, footnoting, and automatic tables of contents and indexes. All good programs now work with mouse control, pull-down menu windows, and on-line help.

B. *Desktop Publishing*

Many advanced word processing programs permit you to combine text and graphics in documents and print "camera-ready" results on laser printers. Still more advanced programs provide complete writing, design, and production tools you can use to create professional-quality publications that are excellent for school news communications and the like. Some programs also provide comprehensive and powerful layout and production features that are economical and save valuable administrative time. High-end typographic control and format options also help produce high-quality documents.

Computers with good word processing applications can quickly spoil anyone accustomed to a typewriter and can rival the conventional word processing systems, which are limited to word processing. The main purpose of a computer-based word processing program is to produce hard copy output: letters, reports, and printed materials. For this reason, the printer used to print documents is no doubt the most important component in the system. The word processing program selected should have a wide selection of printer drivers available with extensive selection of character sizes and styles (fonts). Many printers can produce high-quality text and graphics on a single page.

7.5 Spreadsheets and Accounting

The original purpose of computers was to perform numerical calculations. The spreadsheet is a program extension of the computer's calculating capacity. Spreadsheets help busy administrators keep track of elaborate numerical and financial information and scrutinize complex numerical data for management decision making. The spreadsheet is a program that allows the entry of numbers and equations in a free-form manner.

A. School Uses of Spreadsheets

Virtually any calculations that can be done on a sheet of paper can be done automatically through the use of a spreadsheet program. Common applications of spreadsheets include financial analysis, revenue monitoring, data compilation, trends and changes over time, and forecasting. Other applications include record keeping for petty cash accounts, cost-effectiveness analysis, and inventory control. A spreadsheet also can be used to organize numerical information and illustrate summaries or relationships in many creative ways. For example, note in the sample spreadsheet in Figure 7.1 (from an actual school district) how a decline in enrollment is contradicted with an increase in budget during a three-year period.

A spreadsheet is like a sheet of columnar paper consisting of rows and columns labeled for ease of location and identification. The size of a spreadsheet depends upon the amount of memory in the computer and the amount of information included. Each spreadsheet cell can hold text, a value, a formula, or a set of instructions, and each cell has an "address." For example, in Figure 7.1, the cell at the intersection of column E and row 6 ("address: E6") contains the district enrollment for 1991-1992 of 7,771 pupils.

B. Spreadsheet Relationships and Forecasting

Because the values in one cell may depend on the value in another cell, the spreadsheet is good for forecasting—doing "what if" analyses. Values in one cell can be changed, and the immediate effects on values in other cells may be seen. This "ripple" effect helps quickly answer questions involving complex mathematical models. For example, in the sample spreadsheet above, cell F7 is programmed to change automatically if the number of pupils changes in cell F6.

The large memory capabilities available on desktop computers allow for the construction of extremely complex and powerful spreadsheet models. The improved performance of newer, more powerful computers speeds up the sizable numbers of

A	B	C	D	E	F
1	School Year	1989-90	1990-91	1991-92	Mean
2	Total district budget	$45,952,593	$49,307,593	$53,900,709	$49,720,298
3	Change from prior year	3.34%	7.30%	9.32%	6.65%
4	District tax rate	100.25	110.12	113.37	107.91
5	District tax valuation	$458,379,980	$447,762,377	$475,440,672	$460,527,677
6	District enrollment	8,056	8,018	7,771	7,948
7	Change from prior year	−3.18%	−0.47%	−3.08%	−2.25%

Figure 7.1. Sample Spreadsheet With School Financial and Enrollment Data

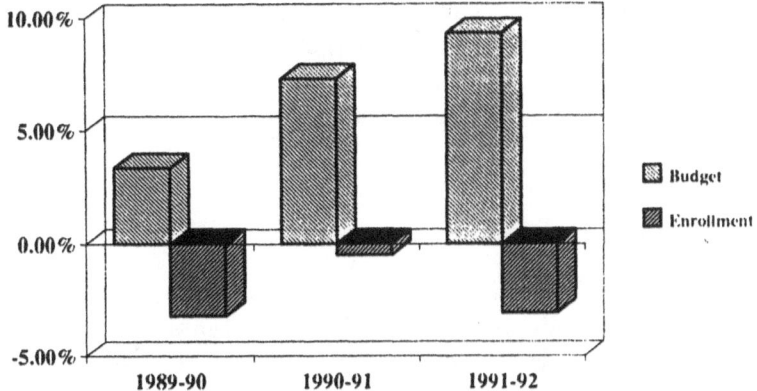

Figure 7.2. Comparisons of Budget and Enrollment Change in Percentages 1989-1992

calculations associated with large spreadsheets. Math coprocessor options speed up these calculations even more.

c. Spreadsheet Graphs and Charts

Some spreadsheet applications are integrated with graphics and can generate high-quality graphs and charts of data. Figure 7.2 is an example of this capability: The spreadsheet is shown in graphic form, and the graph clearly shows the contradictory trends of enrollment and budget levels.

Spreadsheets are used routinely in financial accounting, school district assessment and testing analyses, enrollment monitoring and projecting, and mathematical-based operations.

7.6 Data Base Management

Administrators deal with lots of information. The amount of information processed in school administration is immense and difficult to deal with efficiently, unless the information can be organized in a uniform and accessible manner. Data base management systems provide valuable assistance with this burdensome task. An example of the organization of data is found in telephone directories. Names, street addresses, zip codes, telephone numbers, and cities are variables used to organize what often is a voluminous collection of data. Without such organization, finding someone's phone number would be a horrendous task.

A. *How Data Base Management Systems Work*

Schools are faced with the task of compiling, organizing, and using data on students, faculty and staff, parents, classes, facilities, equipment, materials, activities and events, testing programs, and other components of school operations. Data base management application programs are major implements for organizing large amounts of information with computers. Data base management programs usually organize information into files, records, and fields. A file is a set of information, like the phone book. A record is an individual entry, like the person with the phone. Fields are individual components of the record, such as name, address, and phone number. The entire collection of files, records, and fields is the data base itself.

B. *School Uses of Data Bases*

School administrators can make good use of data base programs for very practical, ordinary needs. Once data are organized and entered into the computer, they can be retrieved quickly and easily. Data bases can hold information about almost anything related to school operations. Sample uses might be updating substitute teacher rosters, flagging at-risk students, sorting library fines by student, and managing a volunteer parent program.

Information from data bases also can be used for integration into other applications, such as merging names and addresses from a data base into routine correspondence. Also, several persons (if authorized) may access the same data base, make or modify entries, and maintain the data as required. Reports and profiles of data are easily obtained and can be excellent tools for decision making. More powerful data base application programs also provide capabilities for the administrator to develop custom programs in easy-to-use language and procedures to employ the school data base environment in unique ways.

c. Storage of Data Bases

Large fixed disks on modern desktop computers provide enough storage for large data bases. For example, one 20-megabyte fixed disk can hold a data base of more than a quarter million records (names and addresses). Floppy diskettes may also be used to store data from data bases, with a 3.5-inch diskette holding more than 10,000 name and address records. High-speed modern computers with advanced operating systems significantly help speed up data base activities.

7.7 Graphics Presentation, Painting, and Drawing

Since prehistoric man sketched on the walls of caves, images have been powerful communication devices. Images are able to convey information in enjoyable ways, and the more information to convey, the more need for graphic representations. It's not surprising, then, that educators rely on images to convey meaning to students, parents, teachers, staff, and community patrons. With the increased use of computers, it is also not surprising to note that computer-generated images, or computer graphics, are common in today's educational environment.

A. *Graphics in School Administration*

Graphics application programs provide the administrator with tools to construct images with a computer. Graphics can be used for comparing enrollments, comparing test data results, depicting energy cost trends, illustrating dropout trends, and comparing grade distributions. These images can be presented as stand-alone presentations or can be incorporated into other work, such as word processing documents. Graphics programs enhance instructional presentations and enliven teaching activities with creative concepts. Programs that are useful for

Figure 7.3. Graphics Example

schools vary widely in price and function, but most products have much to offer the educational user. An example of a graphic produced by a computer program is provided in Figure 7.3.

Some graphics products accept numerical information and create representative graphs, bar charts, or pie charts, even in three-dimensional form. Others provide free-form drawing tools, limited only by the user's imagination.

The package may also include clip art libraries with images such as animals, people, buildings, trees, symbols, maps, or even cartoon characters. Other packages permit scanning images from publications and editing of the image, including photographs. Text can be incorporated into the graphic image.

Once an image is defined, it can be printed, incorporated into a media presentation with slides, or saved on disk. Some programs even allow repair of damaged photographic images with computer operations, and some programs provide automated presentations on a computer screen complete with animation.

B. *Choosing a Graphics Program*

Graphics programs should let you create formatted word charts and data-driven numerical or financial charts. Drawing tools should be provided for designing diagrams, creating images, and drawing artwork. Vector graphics files should be importable, and it is also useful to have the capability to produce 35-mm slides, overhead transparencies, and printed output. It is useful to have large libraries of clip art and pictures for use in documents and publications. Good programs export charts and drawings to common file formats so that they can be incorporated into word-processed or desktop-published documents. Color capabilities are becoming more common as well, and complex effects are available like warping text, simulating 3-D with perspective, and blending between colors and shapes.

"A picture is worth a thousand words" and, with graphics programs, school administrators can successfully edit and illustrate concepts to inform, teach, and perhaps even entertain many different audiences.

7.8 Communications

A communications program is an application that ties other applications or computers together. The simplest job of communications programs is to move information or images from one computer to another.

A. *Functions in Telecommunications*

With computer communications programs, the administrator can communicate with other employees, state agencies, on-line data services (such as *CompuServe* and *Prodigy*, which have educator forums), businesses, board members, even school districts across the country. For example, communications programs allow documents generated by word processing, or images generated by graphics programs, to be sent electronically anywhere in the school district or world in seconds.

Advantageous functions in computer communications include data sharing, program sharing, equipment sharing, electronic messaging, information dissemination, and organizational management.

B. Telecommunications in Administration

Electronic mail services or bulletin boards are very useful in large school systems. They permit exchange of information within an organization without having to play "phone tag" while trying to contact someone. Many computers have fax machine capabilities built in the computer, permitting the sending and receiving of facsimile reproductions of documents. Communications requires a modem (modulator-demodulator) card in the computer with software to manage the requirements.

In some states, administrators can get information about administrative tasks from colleagues. In Iowa, new superintendents have an electronic network for communicating with experienced superintendents by computer. Questions and answers can be either privately shared or posted publicly for others to read.

Many administrators have lap-top or portable computers for working away from the office. With a modem, files and work can be downloaded or uploaded from the portable computer to the office computer over phone lines. With phone lines, modem, and software, any computer can become a terminal for any other computer. Local area networks also provide many benefits to the school organization, even small school districts.

School administrators cherish accurate, timely, and manageable information. If there is one important activity in any school district, it is the act of getting important information to the right decision maker. Available information determines choices that can have far-reaching effects on the success of the school. Improve communications in schools, and productivity and efficiency will improve accordingly.

7.9 Programs and Application Development

Many general-purpose application programs have been developed by schools to perform various tasks. One of the simplest variations of the above application programs is to combine several of the functions into an integrated or all-in-one application or program. There are integrated programs that combine spreadsheets, word processing, data base management, and communications all into one package, such as *First Choice* (Software Publishing) or *Works* (Microsoft).

Another approach has been to provide a series of programs designed to work together. The series approach permits the user to select only the programs needed for the task at hand. For example, a separate word processing program can be used independently. In graphics user interface environments (as used in Microsoft *Windows* or Apple Macintosh programs), however, the user can move information from one program to another. For example, information from a spreadsheet can be moved into a word processing document. Such file exchange capabilities are very useful in complex work projects, such as reports to the board of education or the public on school financial needs.

A. *School Custom Program Applications*

Many school administrators find that commercially available software is inadequate for their needs in specific tasks. Custom-made software may be required. Many states require school administrators to use standard accounting systems, but the systems may not meet local needs in managing data. Other special tasks such as handling comprehensive teacher evaluation data for a large number of teachers may require unique programs. In such cases, the administrator is well advised to develop individually personalized applications.

Programming a computer is not easy; therefore custom application programs are commonly written by programmers or outside consulting firms. Fortunately, many ready-made programs are available for tailoring applications to the school administrator's needs. Many products offer data base management or spreadsheet programming options, and these are often useful but complex. Other off-the-shelf products provide easy-to-use programs that help the school administrator design and implement his or her own applications with a minimum of study and time.

TABLE 7.2 Custom Programmable Applications For Schools

Program Name	Features	Publisher
Professional File	Inexpensive, very easy to use, practical operations	Software Publishing Co.
Alpha Four	Moderate cost, easy to use, reasonably powerful operations	Alpha Software, Inc.
dBase IV	Expensive, difficult to use, very powerful operations	Ashton-Tate Co.

In just a few hours, an administrator may design a program application, pilot test its features, and implement it effectively. Some of the applications that can be designed and created by the administrator include accounting, mailing lists, student records, bibliographies, inventory records, data collection and analysis, personnel tracking, and other information management.

Many of the custom program applications are menu driven and designed to enable the school administrator to create some programs that in the past required the services of a professional programmer. Data from these programmable operations are usually transportable to other formats. Examples of these custom programmable applications are shown in Table 7.2.

B. *Application Generators (Hypermedia)*

The first "hypermedia" program to popularize creation of applications was Apple Computer's *Hypercard*. That program lets Macintosh users retrieve and link information using an index card-type system. Now there are several hypertext (hypermedia-based) packages available for DOS-based (or IBM-compatible) computers, many with advanced features such as text linking, action linking, and linking to other programs. Some recently introduced programs are listed in Table 7.3.

TABLE 7.3 Programmable Applications

Type	Programs	Features
Application generators	*Linkway* (IBM Corporation) *Hypercard* (Apple Macintosh) *Hyperpad* (Brightbill-Roberts)	Index card-like information linking
Development language programs	*Knowledge Engine* (Software Artistry) *Knowledgepro* (Knowledge Garden)	Language-based text links, program links
Personal information developers	*Grandview* (Symantec) *Memory Mate* (Broderbund)	Link references (two pieces of information)
Expert writing programs	*1st Class HT* (1st Class Expert Systems) *Personal Consultant Plus* (Texas Instruments)	Using embedded bases of expert knowledge with problem-solving capabilities (very expensive)

There are many ways for associative linking and nonlinear writing and reading to be used in school administration. The most powerful use lies in the potential of these programs to help in writing electronic training programs, instructional activities, electronic manuals, and other large text and graphics-based applications. Staff development trainers and curriculum development personnel especially would find these programs useful.

7.10 Selecting Computer Hardware

Computers come in all shapes and sizes, speeds, and costs. School administrators want a machine they can use, one that will perform the functions they need, and one they can afford. Several factors affect the hardware selection that is best for a particular school administrative setting.

Fortunately, there are some givens. First, it is assumed that the school administrator is interested in a personal computer; that is, one that can be located on a desktop and easily accessed by the user. Mainframes and minicomputers do not quite fill the bill in this case. Second, the computer cost should fit the budget of the administrator. Computers are available from $1,000 up to $20,000 or more, but a fully functional system is obtainable for $3,000 to $5,000, including all components described in this chapter. Third, the sophistication of a computer appropriate for the school environment is well within the stated price range. In fact, the power and potency of computers in this range usually exceeds, by many times, the capability of the owner to employ the full extent of its capabilities. As you gain in experience and confidence, however, you will easily harness more and more of the computer's power.

A. *Components of Computer Systems*

The process of selecting a computer system comes down to making decisions about five essential components. These decisions can be made by the administrator without professional help, given clear expectations for the work that is to be performed. The five essential components are (a) operating systems, (b) input devices, (c) processor types, (d) storage capacities, and (e) output devices.

Operating systems. Selection of the operating system depends upon many factors:

- Simultaneous, multiple applications or single-application use
- Multiple users or single user
- Operating memory needs for software
- Compatibility with other applications and programs
- Graphics user interface environment preferences
- System architecture: proprietary or publicly shared
- Range and availability of applications and programs
- Popularity and durability of market demand

TABLE 7.4 Operating System Distribution

Operating System	1989 10 Million Units %	1994 17.8 Million Units %
IBM-DOS	75.0	43.2
Windows-DOS	14.5	28.7
OS/2	1.7	13.5
UNIX	2.3	7.6
Macintosh	6.5	7.0

SOURCE: Data from LaPlante (1991, p. 64)

The market share for operating systems in use in the United States in 1989 and projected for 1994 is shown in Table 7.4. Each system listed presents the school administrator with advantages and disadvantages. All have pros and cons for use in school environments. Administrators will need to become acquainted with the features and capabilities of each before purchase. With the data exchange options that are now available, however, the choice of operating system may not be as critical as it once was.

Input devices. Computers don't act on their own initiative. They need to be "told" what to do. Until voice command devices are available, the computer must receive instructions and data from its human operator in other ways. The devices that allow the operator to direct the computer are known as "input devices." Keyboards, scanners, and pointing devices (the mouse and variations), are each useful and, in the case of the keyboard, essential. The choice should be guided by personal preference and considerations of intended use, function, price, and dependability.

Processors. The microprocessor is the brain of the computer, and it is the organ that does the real work. It interprets program instructions, performs calculations and logical operations, and controls other parts of the computer. Processors are grouped according to speed and capacity. The microchips that are the workhorse of the processor are rated as to the individual binary digits, or bits, it can handle simultaneously. Older machines handle 8 bits (or one byte) at a time. Newer machines handle 16 or 32 bits at a time. The greater speed and power of 32-bit machines permit simultaneous use by several operators or manipulation of several applications at the same time. The speed of a computer is stated in megahertz (MHz); the larger the number, the faster the machine.

Storage and capacity. Computer storage, or memory, is necessary to facilitate operation of the microprocessor and store data and instructions until needed. Random access memory (RAM) serves as temporary storage of data, and the capacity (usually stated in megabytes) contributes to the power and capability of the computer. RAM is usually available in 640 K (or .640 megabytes) in older DOS-based machines, and in 1-megabyte combinations in advanced DOS-based or Macintosh computers. At least 2 megabytes of RAM is recommended to operate two or more complex software applications simultaneously.

Permanent, or secondary, storage is provided by different kinds of storage media. After a document is finished, its data and instructions can be saved on a standard fixed disk, micro diskettes, memory expansion cards, tape storage devices, and other storage media. Diskettes are inexpensive and can be exchanged between desktop and portable computers for ease of editing. Exchange of data can also be managed with computer local area networks or cable connections. The 1.44-Mb diskettes now used by most computers can hold more than 750 double-spaced pages of text and fit in your shirt pocket or purse, making it easy to transport long documents.

Hard disk drives store data on hard disks coated with a magnetic substance and can store millions of bytes of data and instructions. Hard disk drives are available in any size capacity, and the typical *Windows*-DOS user will find that 60 Mb of storage or even more will be put to good use.

Computer Technology Functions 151

Output. The results of the microprocessor's work are communicated in a couple of ways, usually to a monitor and sometimes to a storage device or to a printer. Monitors are video display units, not unlike television sets, and they come in monochrome or color styles. The Video Graphics Array (VGA) monitor is currently the most advanced form of video graphics display. Its maximum image colors total 256, while the EGA displays 16 colors, the CGA displays 4 colors, and the MCA (monochrome) displays only black and white. Color has many advantages in graphics and complex applications, but monochrome displays are generally adequate for spreadsheet and ordinary word processing applications.

Modern printers currently in use provide crisp, clear documents of high quality. Printers come in many forms, and the entry-level type is the inexpensive dot-matrix printer, which provides near-letter-quality printing and acceptable graphics. A higher cost level is found with the ink-jet type printers, with costs about twice those of dot-matrix printers. Ink-jet printers provide excellent text printing and graphics. Still better quality is available, at increased cost, with laser printers. Laser printers produce superior graphics and text printing.

B. *Recommended Administrator Computer Equipment*

At the risk of running into rapid obsolescence, it seems appropriate to list the components of a suggested school administrator's office computer system. A general-purpose computer workstation should include the following components for effective and successful school administration and management.

Base system:	386-based (or higher) microprocessor, with 2 Mb of RAM (minimum) or equivalent
Input:	Enhanced keyboard and pointing device (mouse)
Operating system:	*Windows*/DOS-based system or OS/2 or equivalent

Storage:	60-Mb fixed disk drive storage unit (or larger) 3½-inch 1.44 Mb diskette drive plus 5¼-inch drive if exchanging data with older machines)
Monitor:	VGA graphics display
Printer:	Laser printer with full-page print (Postscript) capability (with 2-Mb RAM module)
Peripherals:	Modem (with fax)

Regardless of the type of computer obtained or used, the school administrator is better off with a computer than without one. As is the case with any tool, the quality of school and administrative work is enhanced with the computer. Unless computers are used in schools by administrators, children and teachers will have to look elsewhere for models of excellence in technology applications.

7.11 Moving Schools Into the Technological Future

School classrooms haven't changed much since the turn of the century. Administrators, however, can do much to bring their schools into the future. School administrators who see the value of the computer as a tool and as an enhancement to educational technology are well positioned to develop and implement technological school environments. Some suggestions for moving ahead are delineated below.

Suggestions for Advancing School Quality With Technology

1. Develop a comprehensive vision-based master plan for computer education and use in all phases of your school.

2. Define a curriculum designed in key subject areas at all grade levels for computers and technology.
3. Work to acquire adequate resources for your school's acquisition of sufficient computer equipment.
4. Provide support, inspiration, and staff development on computer uses and instruction to teachers.
5. Select instructional materials and software for computing applications carefully based on sound criteria.
6. Gather up the isolated, unused computers and place them where they will be used.
7. Create and establish short- and long-term courses in computer science subjects.
8. Evaluate the results of your computer program rigorously and use the feedback to improve its delivery.

7.12 Summary

Schools are not likely to change or do anything better without leadership. An effective leader must be a change agent, using modern skills to increase knowledge and learn new strategies. Looking ahead, it is easy to see that computers will be used in new and exciting ways in schools. The possibilities for computer technology in the twenty-first century are limitless, and careful preparation today will produce an environment where students can grow and succeed tomorrow. In the complex future, there is only room for those leaders who move ahead and who enhance the quality of schools with computer technology.

References

American Association of School Administrators. (1990). Connecting our students to the future: Computer technology report [Special issue]. *The School Administrator*.

Dockterman, D. A. (1989). *Teaching in the one computer classroom*. Cambridge, MA: Snyder.

Dvorak, J. C., & Anis, N. (1990). *Dvorak's guide to PC telecommunications*. New York: McGraw-Hill.
Goodman, P. S., Sproull, L. S., et. al. (1990). *Technology and organizations*. San Francisco: Jossey-Bass.
LaPlante, A. (1991, January). Industry outlook. *PC World*, 64.
Richards, C. E. (1989). *Microcomputer applications for strategic management in education*. White Plains, NY: Longman.
Thompson, A. (1990). *Personal applications in computer education*. Dubuque, IA: Kendall/Hunt.

8

School-Based Budgeting for Cost Efficiency and Educational Effectiveness

School transformation and improvement activities have significant budget and management implications. In improving the effectiveness and quality of instruction, you often have to make changes in operations without any corresponding increase in resources. The challenge is to improve the productivity of our schools within existing, or even diminishing, resources. As one discerning teacher once said, "We need to do more with less." Educators have had to make do with little in the way of resources for generations and have done remarkably well under the circumstances.

Perhaps budgeting is not quite that simple, but school improvement is the result of careful planning, particularly in the use of scarce resources. As you and your staff work to budget your financial, human, and technical resources for school quality enhancement, the focus of your activity must be on what you hope to achieve, not what you plan to buy. This chapter aims to provide you with some insights into how productivity is enhanced in use of resources and decision making, how you might choose from several types of budgeting processes, how you can employ principles of quality enhancement in budgeting, and how you can capitalize on the benefits of school-based management.

8.1 Enhancing Productivity in Use of Resources

A productive school system is one that gets better over time, independent of changes in the level of resources available to it. In other words, even if your school were declining in enrollment and financial support, it should be possible to improve performance given certain actions on your part. The trick is to use the tools at your disposal to improve the effectiveness and quality of your school organization's operations and to improve the efficiency of its processes at the same time.

How can you make your school more educationally effective and at the same time more cost-efficient? Primarily, it involves research-based systems with accumulation of hard data, extrapolation of findings, and implementation of action accordingly. As your school organization plans, organizes, implements, and evaluates its activities, it can only get better if it makes adjustments or modifications in its activities as a result of feedback on its performance. If feedback is spotty, flawed, or ignored, productivity is jeopardized. If feedback is comprehensive, thorough, valid, and used in decision making, productivity is enhanced.

If your school organization establishes a solid relationship between what it does and how well it does it, and then uses that link to shape what it does next, your organization will improve in performance. In addition, it should improve in its use of resources, reduce wasteful activity, terminate ineffective programs, and generally get better at what it does over time.

School-Based Budgeting 157

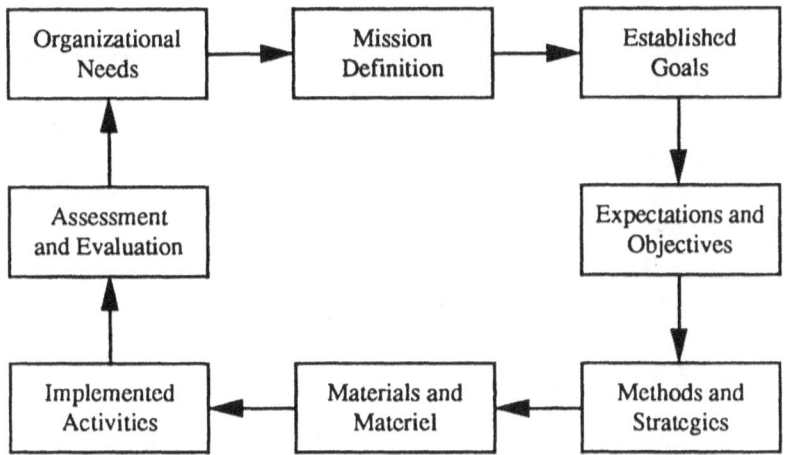

Figure 8.1. Example of a Linear Program Quality Cycle

A. *A Model for Productivity*

One way to look at the development of productivity is by illustrating its components in graphic form, as shown in Figure 8.1. In this illustration, the linear relationship among needs, mission, goals, objectives, methods, material, activities, and feedback is shown.

B. *Steps to Productivity*

In graphic depiction in Figure 8.1, productivity results from progression through specific procedures. For you to improve productivity over time, the steps to follow are simply stated in the following list:

1. Determine your organizational needs, using appropriate needs assessment techniques.
2. Define your organizational mission, or the overall results you want to accomplish.
3. Establish your organizational goals for the next three to five years.
4. Delineate organizational expectations and program objectives.

5. Identify and select from alternative methods and strategies you might employ, including staffing.
6. Develop or select appropriate materials, equipment, or other materiel necessary to do the job.
7. Implement your planned activities in accordance with your decisions to this point.
8. Assess or measure results and performance and apply evaluative judgment.
9. Use feedback in determining organizational needs and cycle through the process again.

c. Cautions and Considerations

Some cautions should be noted here for your guidance. This program quality cycle is considerably boiled down in complexity and scope. For more comprehensive direction in planning and decision making, consult the more complete and useful information found in references at the end of this chapter.

Some conditions for use of this simple decision-making cycle for productivity should also be noted. There are certain administrative precepts you should follow. For example, the collaboration of appropriate parties, generally representatives of affected groups, in decisions is essential. Also, definitions of goals, objectives, mission, and other components must be in measurable terms so you can see clearly whether or not you achieved or reached them. Moreover, feedback needs to be comprehensive and continuous. Evaluation along the way through this process will help you stay on track.

8.2 School-Based Budgeting

School-based decentralized budgeting is another way for school systems to make decisions and allocate resources. The process calls for individuals who implement budgetary decisions to help make those decisions. The idea is to put the decision-making power at the organizational level closest to the decision. In school-based budgeting, the principal, in collaboration with staff and constituents, has been delegated the responsibility to budget resources at the individual building level. Given the discretionary authority to determine how resources are used in a given school, it is believed that people will feel a sense of ownership and commitment for improvement in the activities and programs within their school.

A. *Rationale for School-Based Budgeting*

Given the challenge to improve schools, research has taught us that efficiency and productivity are more likely to flourish with school autonomy than with extensive central control. In the use of resources, quality demands both centralized and decentralized operations, but in different dimensions and with different responsibilities.

Centralization of authority has not always given us the outcomes we wanted in schools. Educational history in recent decades has revealed that the central office has done some things well and has done other things not so well. For example, central direction has been very effective in dealing with issues of justice in equal access to educational opportunity. It has been less effective in dealing with issues of organization and operation of individual schools for instructional quality. Factors associated with effectiveness in instruction are more likely to be found at the individual school level.

Another reason for school-based budgeting is simply that the school is usually the basic cost center in the delivery of educational services. It is the smallest "whole" unit within the greater "whole" of the school system. Moreover, the principal is likely to be the most significant factor in the improvement of instruction. Consequently, the belief is that the school system must be configured to allow individual schools to deal with their own problems—as much as is appropriate.

There is a need for central direction and regulation and for the necessary forms of accountability. The balance that is needed, however, gives individual school units enough flexibility and discretion to effectively deliver their services and products. This balance of responsibility and distribution of authority should foster prudent monitoring and sound execution of districtwide functions at the central level and foster creative and ample autonomy for organizational decision making aimed toward successful attainment of goals and standards at the school level.

B. Central Responsibilities in School-Based Budgeting

There are shared and separate responsibilities in school-based budgeting, and your district will need to decide which is which. The district office, or superintendent and governing board, should have the responsibility to define and disseminate districtwide curriculum expectations and organizational goals. The overall district budget, or spending plan, must be established at the central level, although prudent judgment provides for broad and vertical organizational collaboration in the process.

Capital expenditures, including major maintenance and construction, are best planned and directed from the district level, as are other major districtwide activities, such as energy management, food services, and transportation. Equity and standards in personnel selection generally also must be assured by the district office, including the screening of personnel and the administration of compensation and benefits.

The board and superintendent must have major responsibility in setting policies, developing and implementing regulations and procedures, defining staffing configurations and levels, and managing collective bargaining agreements. In addition, textbooks and overall program tests and assessment procedures and instruments are best selected for districtwide use at the central level. Evaluation of performance against standards is perhaps the most important responsibility the board and superintendent have. Without careful assessment of results, no system has a way of knowing whether or not its expectations are being met.

C. School Responsibilities in School-Based Budgeting

It isn't enough that schools, or building-level administrators, receive increased autonomy and administrative discretion in decision making and organizational operations. In addition, any increase in authority must always be accompanied by an increase in accountability. School-based budgeting doesn't mean that schools have freedom to buy or spend anything they want. Rather, it means that schools have flexibility and greater latitude in decisions about how to allocate the resources designated for their school to best achieve success.

For example, one principal in a large Arizona suburban elementary school was allocated a certain number of teachers by the central office based upon the number of students in the school. The principal and people at that school mutually decided not to hire their full complement of teachers but to use the salary monies of two teaching positions to hire paraprofessionals instead. They were able to hire three or four paraprofessionals to work with individual students for each teaching position they converted. The flip side was that all teachers had to accept a few more students in each classroom because of the resulting increases in class size. Further, the school was just as accountable for the results they received with their locally determined distribution of resources as before.

School-based budgeting also calls for collaborative planning, careful determination of strengths and weaknesses, clearly defined school goals and objectives, training and time to develop processes needed for implementation, and a monitoring system in place at the school level. In addition, different budget development procedures and processes are needed, which are explained later in this chapter.

Autonomy and discretion are two of the prime ingredients for leadership opportunity, and school-based budgeting provides a great setting for its development. You, as the administrator and leader, constantly need to seek new and better ways of doing things, with more cost efficiency, to advance the quality of the learning environment under your direction. You also need support and flexibility, however, for significant school-level budget decisions. Given these factors, school-based budgeting is another tool to help schools match available resources to the needs of their students, develop plans and programs to meet unique goals, and get the best results from their efforts.

8.3 Budgeting Processes and Levels

The basic purpose of a budget is to serve as a guide or plan for the use of financial resources in the management of programs and services. The budget should give you a framework for your school's work toward organizational goals within limited resources and to balance projected expenditures with anticipated revenues. It comes as no surprise to note that budget requests in most school systems generally exceed available financial resources. Of course, several approaches to budgeting are available to schools but, in this chapter, four levels or classifications of budgeting will be considered.

The first, called *formula* (or administrative) budgeting is perhaps the most common in public schools. Less common are *program* budgeting and *incremental* budgeting. Of the four types, the least used process is *performance-based* (sometimes called "curriculum-driven") budgeting (English, 1987).

A. Level I: Formula Budgeting

In formula budgeting, relationships between resources available and cost projections are established. Given a certain level of revenues, a configuration of services, materials, or other commodities is developed and organized in terms of its end use. In other words, its "object of expenditure" is the mode of organization such as salaries, benefits, supplies, and purchased services. In addition, the process is often "closely held," usually by a small policymaking or executive group or individual (superintendent or business official). The executive body reviews revenues and exercises control over the expenditures within defined procedures or formulas. Public or staff involvement in decision making is limited, and it is difficult to track planned expenditures to specific educational objectives or purposes.

B. Level II: Program Budgeting

In program budgeting, the purpose or intended activity of the expenditure is the organizing variable. This level involves organizing and presenting information about costs and benefits of the school's activities related to purposes or goals. Program budgeting establishes connections between programs, services, or activities with plans for allocation of funds. Objectives and goals are established, alternative programs are costed and considered, and allocations are made by choosing among the alternatives to the limit of available resources. In program budgeting, you would be able to find tangible relationships between the school's programs and budget and to identify a planned (and observable) congruence between the purpose of the school and expenditures. Usually, the "function-object" classification of expense from level I is incorporated into level II.

c. Level III: Incremental Budgeting

Incremental budgeting is simply a process in which programs are broken into packages, or increments, costed separately, rank ordered as to preferability, and funded in ordinal fashion up to the limit of available resources. "Zero-based" budgeting falls into this category. Incremental budgeting relies on a program structure, usually is convertible to object format, and involves decision making as to the level or quantity of service for a program. For example, class size could be treated as a program and funded at one of several increment levels, as shown in Table 8.1, taken from a school district in Oregon.

In the example in Table 8.1, class size could be funded from 22 pupils per teacher to 30 pupils per teacher, depending upon how much the decision-making body determined to allocate for this program. It's interesting to note that, in this district of about 25,000 pupils, increasing or reducing the average elementary class size by one pupil adds or subtracts about $1,000,000. This is just one way the process provides you with various decision options. In addition, other program packages (i.e., gifted and talented education, instrumental music, and so on) would be arranged in the same fashion, permitting funding at differential levels or with quantities of each program. In a sense, program increments compete for funding in this process.

TABLE 8.1 Incremental Budgeting: Class Size Example

Package ID	Package Name (with class size)	Package Cost $	Cumulative Cost $
101-01	Elementary instruction 1:30	21,503,032	21,503,032
101-02	Elementary instruction 1:28	2,197,063	23,700,095
101-03	Elementary instruction 1:26	2,109,719	25,809,814
101-04	Elementary instruction 1:24	2,078,887	27,888,701
101-05	Elementary instruction 1:22	2,005,332	29,894,033

D. Level IV: Performance (Curriculum-Driven) Budgeting

Performance budgeting is often called curriculum-driven, data-driven, or results-based budgeting. The underlying nature of performance budgeting is to tie measured performance, or achievement of established outcomes or objectives, into the decision-making process. Funding is based upon the observable value obtained from the program and level. Resources are allocated by program activities, quantity or level, and measurements of results, which link outcomes to resources. The aim is to implement a process that results in a planned budget based upon the measured and defined educational needs and accomplishments of a school system. Assessment data on educational effectiveness, or viability, are used to build the budget, and performance budgets are generally highly collaborative in nature and definitely lean toward decentralized decision making.

E. Comparisons of Budgeting Levels

The four levels described above are graphically illustrated in Table 8.2. The table shows how each level incorporates the fea-

TABLE 8.2 Budget Level Characteristics and Components

Characteristics and Components		Levels			
		I	II	III	IV
Formula/object	(What is purchased?)	x	x	x	x
Purpose/activity	(What is performed?)		x	x	x
Increment/level	(What quantity is provided?)			x	x
Results/performance	(What value is procured?)				x

tures of the lower levels and, in a few words, attempts to describe the nature of each level.

8.4 Implementing School-Based Performance Budgeting

School-based budgeting should provide for allocation of a school's discretionary funds based on assessment data and with participation of key staff members. In this way, it not only can promote greater productivity but can promote teamwork and commitment on the part of members of the organization as well. School-based budgeting uses the individual school's educational programs as the framework for planning and places the school's administrator right in the middle of the budgeting process. The specific configuration of the process depends upon many factors, particularly the capability of the system to define and measure quality and equity.

Quality can be measured in many different ways. For example, one school district evaluated the reading achievement levels of its elementary schools, finding considerable discrepancy and wide differences. The range of difference is shown in Figure 8.2.

In this example, reading achievement ranges from a norm curve equivalent score of 28 to a high of 83. Despite such discrepancy in achievement levels among schools, the school system

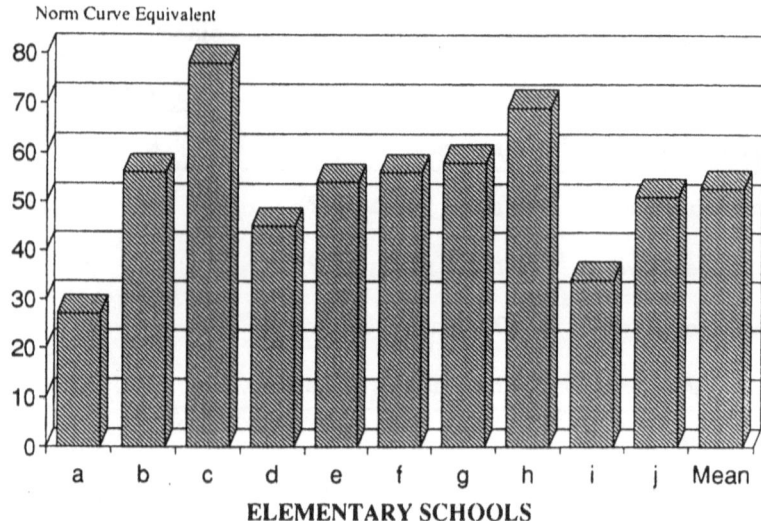

Figure 8.2. Mean Achievement Comparisons (reading, grades K-3, ITBS, 1991)

had for years allocated staff resources uniformly to all of its schools. This resulted in each school receiving a formula allocation of one reading specialist for each 400 pupils. Because most elementary schools had 900 students, each school received two specialists. After reviewing the assessment data, it was determined that allocation by enrollment was inequitable, and the assignment of reading specialists was changed. Specialists were assigned on the basis of measured pupil performance and differential needs in the reading program. Some schools received a part-time specialist, other schools received two or more specialists, depending upon distance from the district mean. Schools achieving below the mean received additional reading specialist time; schools above the mean received less services. This is one example of a performance-driven budget decision.

In performance budgeting, if guidelines and assigned responsibilities aren't properly worked out, problems can result. For example, one educational writer offered many proposals, some highly questionable, for school-based management. Among these were the suggestion that selection of textbooks be handled by individual schools and that reallocation of funds be permitted within a school regardless of source. Such reckless statements fail to recognize the inviolability of categorical funding (such as Chapter 1 or other federal programs) or to acknowledge major standards of quality control in curriculum management within a school system. It wouldn't make sense to have several different textbooks at a given grade level in a school system, any more than it would make sense to have several different curriculums. Another statement called for school principals to be accountable for energy costs within their schools. This would cause shivers among principals of schools built before energy consciousness changed the way schools were designed. As you can see, some common sense is called for in carefully delegating responsibilities for school-based budgeting.

A. *General Budgeting Factors*

Several factors need to be considered in budgeting, and budgets must be prepared after a full examination and evaluation of each dimension. Factors to be considered include the following:

1. *Purpose and intended outcomes of each program:* What does the program intend to accomplish?
2. *Alternative activities and procedural options*: What different ways can the outcomes be reached?
3. *Personnel requirements—professional and support:* What are the human resource requirements?
4. *Materiel requirements—supplies and equipment:* What are the things needed to do the job?
5. *Space and environmental requirements:* What conditions or facilities are required?
6. *Assessment results from previous budget cycles*: What has worked before?
7. *Cost projections for subsequent years:* What cost alternatives are available?
8. *Time requirements and scheduled flow of events*: What are the reasonable time requirements?

After information is obtained relative to the factors in budgeting, the planning process may begin. Certain assumptions should guide the planning.

B. *Performance Budgeting Assumptions*

Certain assumptions underlie budgeting for productivity. Focusing on the precepts of level IV budgeting described previously, the process should be guided by the following assumptions:

1. Curriculum and instructional program outcomes can be defined.
2. Levels in achievement of programs may be identified and measured.
3. Results from assessment can be translated into program needs.
4. Needs and program priorities change over time.
5. Program needs can be expressed as budget requests.
6. Budget requests generally exceed available financial resources.
7. Assessment data and feedback should direct establishment of priorities.
8. Budget decisions should be driven by curriculum and program requirements and value.

C. *Elements in Performance Budgeting*

As to how the process can be best implemented at the school level, several elements must be incorporated within curriculum-driven budgeting. These elements in the process include the following:

1. Budget requests should be built in incremental, programmatic form.
2. Principals and teachers must be active participants in the budget planning decisions.
3. Costs and benefits of budget requests must be delineated clearly.

4. Priorities must be rank ordered by a school-based decision-making body.
5. Requests must publicly compete for funding priority.
6. Tangible evidence of program results must guide allocations.

Considering the above elements, it is easy to distill the performance budget into three basic characteristics, or hallmarks.

D. Hallmarks of a Performance Budget

There are three hallmarks of a performance, or curriculum-driven, budget. First, the developmental planning process preceding the budget must be participatory. That is, those who are affected by the budget decisions would be a part of the decision-making process. Submission of requests and justification of needs are not enough. Unless teachers and principals are involved in the actual budget decision-making process, the process cannot hope to be valid.

Second, the decision-making process would be public and open to scrutiny by others, especially parents and patrons. This calls for a format that is easily understood and well disseminated throughout the process. In the best of cases, even very large budgets can be presented in just a few pages in highly readable, comprehensive form, revealing ample program and performance information.

Third, budget ingredients should comprise increments, or pieces, of programs. These levels, or increments, can facilitate rank ordering on the basis of measured needs, demonstrated costs and benefits, and assessment results. Given these three hallmarks, the performance budget process enables you to be in sound position to properly allocate funds or resources to carry out the system's needs and programs in priority order.

8.5 Moving Toward Performance Budgeting

Once your school has put the system and tools together to link goals and performance feedback, it will be possible to move ahead with performance budgeting. Remember that it's critical that organizational goals, objectives, activities, and programs must be evaluated and reviewed, on the basis of results and cost, by a team of school personnel. Recommendations for budgeting must be independent of previous budget and program allocations and must not be recurrences of previous-year formulas or decisions. Major steps for moving toward performance budgeting are delineated in the following section.

A. *Develop Programmatic Units*

Begin by identifying various educational activities or programs within your school and group them into broad areas of like need, similarity of service, or commonality of purpose. Exclude all programs that are handled at other levels in the organization, such as textbook selection, utilities, and transportation. An example might be "instruction—class size." Other examples might include "library services, student activities, custodial services, instrumental music," and so on. Program units should be about 25-40 in number. Having too many units complicates the decision process unnecessarily.

B. *Build Unit Increments*

Within each programmatic unit, you should build increments or "packages" that provide varying levels of allocation (increasing or decreasing) from some standard. For example, you might use last year's funding level as a standard and then develop several levels of funding above and below the standard. In this example, which is illustrated in Table 8.3, if last year's budget provided library staffing sufficient to keep the library open four days a week, packages or increments could be built above or below that level and costed accordingly.

Program increments should be reasonable in number, but providing not more than five or six for each program unit is preferred for ease of management of the system.

TABLE 8.3 Budget Unit Increments

Increment Title	Description	Cost $
Library services: minimal	Professional staff provided two days per week	15,000
Library services: current	Professional staff provided four days per week	30,000
Library services: optimal	Professional staff provided five days per week	37,500
Library services: augmented	Staff for small group and individual instruction	52,500

c. Configure Increment Packages

Each increment needs four things to be useful in the budget process. First, each increment needs a goal statement or objective, which defines what purpose it serves in measurable and operational terms. The goal or objective must be concise, easily understood, and have the ability to deliver services if funded by itself. In other words, if funded at the increment's level, it must be able to stand alone and deliver a workable program or services within its cost allocation. Second, each increment must have a break-out and compilation of the delivery requirements to support the proposed activities, with full description and all accompanying costs. If the increment is class size, then teacher salaries, benefits, classroom quantities, and so on are examples of things to be compiled and described. Third, each increment must have a defined cost, which describes what it will take to fund the increment independent of other increments. Last, each increment must have a report or digest of performance data, if it has been operating previously, or proposed strategies for measuring its accomplishment, if newly developed. Organizational consequences, outcomes, or results should be clear from the evaluation data, whether the increment will or will not be funded.

D. Develop Decision-Making Process

Guidelines and procedures for decision making must be established prior to implementation. The people who will be involved in the process should make recommendations as to how the process should proceed. Some guidelines used in other settings have included a number of useful items. For example, preparation of "catalog"-type collections of program unit descriptions have been useful in keeping track of many different units and increments. Also, cost information in traditional line item format has been useful for later conversion to standard budget reporting and accounting systems. Rules about assessment data have been helpful in narrowing down the breadth and scope of information that must be analyzed in detail later. In addition, the method by which units and increments will be rated and ranked by the decision-making body is a function that should be given considerable thought and definition beforehand.

E. Ranking Units and Increments

The most important task in the process is to rank order unit increments in priority order, based upon the democratic decision-making process and appropriate use of performance data. Descriptive information about the nature of a unit increment, its purpose and objective, its previous or proposed level of performance, and its cost are a few of the variables considered in the process. After increments are evaluated by the group and judged as to value or efficacy, they are ranked in order of preference. Several consensus-building processes are available for this purpose. An example, showing only an excerpt, of a ranking configuration is illustrated in Table 8.4.

Given the rank ordering described above, you will have a tentative budget listing of unit increments in order of ranked priority.

F. Develop Proposed Budget

Once you have the individual increments of the budget rank ordered, final development of the budget depends upon monies

School-Based Budgeting

TABLE 8.4 Rank Ordered Budget Increments

Rank	Unit-Increment Description	Cost $	Cumulative Cost $
67	Library media: collection expansion 1 book/student	14,123	3,954,797
68	Guidance services: increase staff ratio to 1:325	31,108	3,985,905
69	Instrumental music: move start to grade 4	7,889	3,993,794
70	Custodial service: schedule to 3 cleanings/week	9,224	4,003,018
71	Teacher assistance program: 2 hours/week/teacher	13,665	4,016,683

appropriated and higher-level reviews and decisions. The nice thing about the system is that available revenues might fluctuate up or down but, wherever the funding line is drawn, the increments to be included in the budget have been determined. If the revenues increase, more unit increment packages are funded. If revenues decrease, fewer unit increment packages are funded. In both cases, changes in monies available are handled in accordance with the predetermined priority order. In the ranked table above, if the school has $3,955,000 appropriated, package rank 67 is funded. If the school has $4,020,000 appropriated, then package rank 71 is funded as are all packages with a higher ranking (but lower number).

G. Implement and Evaluate Budget

Within the budget system, both the process and the outcomes are monitored simultaneously. The allocation process must be scrutinized and improved over time. Also, the outcomes of the budget must also be evaluated for future planning and budget decisions. Finances and programs must be analyzed and maintained or modified in accordance with their resultant levels of success. Given this approach to budgeting, you'll find that questions focus more on "how well are we doing?" rather than on "how much did we spend last year?" Central management, the public, and your school team will have a more complete idea of what is (and what is not) funded in operations in your school. In addition, tangible linkages between program results, objectives, and costs will be apparent to all parties concerned. It will be far easier for you to explain why certain portions of the budget are increasing (or decreasing) from year to year.

Implementing the process usually requires three to four years of effort, with continuous revision of procedures and process based on findings and outcomes.

8.6 Organizational Benefits of Performance Budgeting

You'll find that certain organizational advantages accrue to your school organization as a result of using curriculum-driven, or performance, budgeting. Some of the major benefits have been identified and are defined below.

A. *Credibility*

A credible rationale is used for allocation of scarce resources. Limited economic, human, or materiel resources are brought into alignment with organizational goals on a rational basis. Organizational goals are funded in order of importance or perceived value in a reasonable, democratic process.

B. *Feedback*

Assessment feedback is used effectively in budget decisions. Objectives and results are brought into focus, relationships are used in planning, and measurement of efficacy is used in decision making.

C. Ownership

Participation in the budget planning and decision-making process by all members of the school team helps contribute to the acceptance of and commitment to final budget decisions. Such involvement undergirds and fosters corporate ownership of organizational processes and shared values.

D. Communication

Public visibility, team involvement, and an easy-to-understand format enables thorough public knowledge of district operations, goals, and program requirements. Such factors often have been associated with public trust and confidence in public schools.

E. Efficiency

Given competition for resources on a sound basis, efficiency improves. Duplication of effort is diminished, ineffective programs or strategies are terminated or modified, and low-priority or unnecessary activities are eliminated.

F. Creativity

Creative thinking and problem solving are a key part of the budget process. Standard or traditional ways of doing things are subjected to scrutiny and evaluation, and divergent thinking that produces new and better ways of doing things is encouraged.

8.7 Summary

School-based management requires many effective tools to obtain productivity in school organizations. Performance or curriculum-driven techniques offer you new and powerful tools in your quest for productivity. They offer you new tools to use for the complex and difficult management responsibility of budgeting. Of course, it requires your willingness to function within certain procedures, which may be significantly different than your customary or traditional processes. Given your commitment to make performance budgeting work properly, however, it offers you higher productivity, fosters better organizational unity, and holds promise for improved performance in your school programs and activities. The upshot is that you can gain greater educational effectiveness with scarce or limited resources.

References

American Association of School Administrators, National Association of Elementary School Principals, and National Association of Secondary School Principals. (1988). *School-based management: A strategy for better learning.* Washington, DC: AASA Publications.

Cuban, L. (1988). *The managerial imperative and the practice of leadership in schools.* Albany: State University of New York Press.

English, F. W. (1987). *Curriculum management for schools, colleges, business.* Springfield, IL: Charles C Thomas.

Goodlad, J. I. (1984). *A place called school: Prospects for the future.* New York: McGraw-Hill.

Poston, W. K. (1990). Curriculum driven budgeting: Case study of a recent approach to quality control. *National Forum of Educational Administration and Supervision Journal, 7*(2), 59-69.

Poston, W. K. (1991, January). *Curriculum-driven budgeting: Using educational priorities in school budgets.* Paper presented at a seminar of the National Academy for School Executives, San Diego, CA.

Swanson, A. D., & King, R. A. (1991). *School finance: Its economics and politics.* New York: Longman.

Wood, R. C. (Ed.). (1986). *Principles of school business management.* Reston, VA: Association for School Business Officials.

Troubleshooting Guide

Ancillary Services
- Planning for ancillary or support operations   44

Architect Selection
- Selecting architectural firms objectively   118

At-Risk Student Programs and Services
- Accessing programs for widely diverse students   35
- Coping with absenteeism and tardiness   27
- Grouping options with at-risk populations   29
- Team approaches in at-risk student programming   32

Budget Processes and Levels
- Comparing budget types and levels   162
- Differentiating among types of budget processes   165

Community Relationships
- Forming school-business partnerships   4
- Planning for beneficial results in community relationships   7

- Taking action for good school-community relations   3

Computer Communications
- Enhancing administration with telecommunications   144

Computer Hardware Selection
- Planning administrative configurations of computers   151
- Selecting computer hardware for schools   147

Computer Program Options
- Finding and using custom program applications   145
- Identifying types of applications and programs for schools   130
- Selecting software for instructional delivery   133

Computer Technology in Schools
- Moving schools forward into technology   152
- Using computer technology in schools   126

Curriculum-Driven Budgeting
(*see also* **Performance Budgeting**)
- Definition   164

Data Base Management
- Using data bases in school management   139

Discipline
- Gaining schoolwide consistency in discipline   101
- Overcoming inconsistency in enforcement of rules   98

Energy Management
- Conserving energy for economy   122

Enterprise Operations
- Operating money-making programs in schools   57

Facilities, Educational
- Acquiring and using design services and architects   116

- Evaluating adequacy in appraisal of school facilities | 113
- Evaluating function and impact of school facilities | 112
- Planning educational specifications | 114
- Using and managing facilities to build educational quality | 111

Food Services
- Administering a sound food service program | 53
- Establishing a sound counting and claiming system | 55
- Planning meals to meet requirements | 53

Foundations and External Funding
- Enhancing partnerships for greater support | 10
- Expanding financial support with foundations | 59

Graphics Presentations
- Choosing graphics programs | 142
- Using computer graphics in school administration | 141

Grouping for Instruction
- Avoiding detrimental tracking options | 29
- Breaking away from "lockstep" schedules | 35
- Cooperative learning strategies | 32
- Organizing time in paired blocks | 30

Instructional Materials—Challenges and Critics
- Coping with critics and questions on materials | 90

Instructional Materials Evaluation
- Conducting "Kid-Ratings" | 88
- Evaluating and ranking published materials | 83
- Selecting the best publisher | 89

Library Standards and Management
- Priorities in operating a school library | 93

Maintenance and Custodial Services
- Caring for facilities and resources | 119

- Fulfilling maintenance responsibilities — 120
- Supervising custodial services — 122

Office Management
- Organizing the office for efficiency — 48
- Streamlining records and reports — 47

Organizing Schools for Achievement
- Evaluating administrative actions — 40
- Using volunteers to expand achievement — 15

Performance Budgeting
- Defining performance budgeting — 169
- Implementing performance budgeting — 165
- Measuring benefits of performance budgeting — 174
- Moving toward performance budgeting — 164

Privatization of School Operations
- Getting services from the private sector — 59
- When to avoid privatization — 62
- When to consider privatization — 60

Productivity in Education
- Cautions and considerations in use of resources — 158
- Taking steps to greater productivity in school operations — 157

Public Information Dissemination
- Building shared vision and communications — 17
- Unique communications strategies with the public — 18

Publisher Relationships
- Avoiding bias with publishers — 83
- Dealing with publisher representatives — 85
- Negotiating and contracting with publishers — 87

Rewards and Recognition
- Avoiding ineffective reward and recognition actions — 99
- Improving reward and recognition programs — 101

Troubleshooting Guide

Risk Management
- Assuming risks facing your school — 46
- Avoiding risks facing your school — 45
- Calculating risks facing your school — 45
- Insuring against risks facing your school — 47
- Reducing risks around your school — 46
- Transferring risks away from your school — 46

Safe and Orderly Schools
- Achieving consensus on rules — 99
- Deciding how to obtain a safe and secure school — 97
- Evaluating critical areas of safety — 106
- Gaining schoolwide consistency in discipline — 98

Scheduling Instructional Time
- Auditing school learning time — 26
- Extending learning with instructional scheduling — 25

School-Based Budgeting
- Deciding whether to use school-based budgeting — 159
- Fulfilling responsibilities of school-based budgeting — 160
- Implementing school-based budgeting — 161

School Climate
- Building communication for public support — 3
- Building spirit and vigor in the student body — 107
- Creating a safe and secure school — 97
- Getting a cohesive, supportive school climate — 108

Selection of Instructional Materials
- Assuring selected materials will work — 87
- Getting and keeping an objective committee — 66
- Planning selection processes — 65
- Presenting recommendations to the school board — 89

Spreadsheets and Accounting
- Analyzing data with spreadsheets — 136
- Using spreadsheet programs in schools — 137

Textbook Selection
- Managing the textbook selection process — 68
- Using rating systems to narrow choices — 74

Transportation Services
- Maintaining vehicles and safety — 52
- Managing your duties, policies, and operational control — 51
- Supervising drivers — 52

Volunteer Programs and Alternative Staffing
- Gaining additional help in key support areas — 11
- Increasing limited instructional resources with volunteers — 13
- Setting up and operating a volunteer program — 15

Word Processing and Desktop Publishing
- Publishing with desktop applications — 136
- Selecting a word processing program — 135

Notes

Notes

Notes

Notes

Notes

NOTES

In compliance with GPSR, should you have any concerns about the safety of this product, please advise: International Associates Auditing & Certification Limited The Black Church, St Mary's Place, Dublin 7, D07 P4AX Ireland
EUAR@ie.ia-net.com

www.ingramcontent.com/pod-product-compliance
Lightning Source LLC
Chambersburg PA
CBHW031416290426
44110CB00011B/400